DRINK YOUR OWN GARDEN

DRINK YOUR OWN GARDEN

A HOMEBREW GUIDE USING YOUR GARDEN INGREDIENTS

JUDITH GLOVER

BATSFORD

This edition first published in the United Kingdom in 2013 by
Batsford
10 Southcombe Street
London W14 0RA

First published in 1979 by Batsford
Revised in 2013 by Ted Bruning

An imprint of Anova Books Company Ltd

Copyright © Batsford, 2013

ISBN: 9781849940627

A CIP catalogue record for this book is available from
the British Library.

20 19 18 17 16 15 14 13
10 9 8 7 6 5 4 3 2 1

Reproduction by Mission Productions Ltd, Hong Kong
Printed by 1010 Printing International Ltd, China

This book can be ordered direct from the publisher at the website:
www.anovabooks.com, or try your local bookshop.

CONTENTS

INTRODUCTION

I opened my front door one winter morning and found lying outside it a cardboard box, heavy with what turned out to be parsnips. There was no mystery about the origin of this gift: a neighbour who has an allotment grows more than his family can consume, and kindly distributes the surplus to friends.

I'm very partial to baked parsnips, but not for three meals a day for a week, which is about what it would have taken to get through this offering. So it occurred to me to try making the excess parsnips into wine. I borrowed a library book about the process, bought the minimum of necessary equipment and materials, and had a go. It proved easier and less time-consuming than I'd imagined, except for the period afterwards when I wasted hours, hypnotised by what was going on in the fermenting jar and counting the seconds between the rhythmical bubbling of the air-lock.

In fact, it was an anti-climax when the visible working ceased and I had to leave the process to its less dramatic stages. So I bought another jar, and a couple of pounds of in-season carrots, and set another gallon of liquid into foaming activity. Within a month or so the spare room contained a whole line of jars of contents of differing hues, their air-locks sounding away at different rates.

In due course the contents were racked and later siphoned into bottles (with a certain sampling of the raw wine as part of the job), and laid down in the cellar to mature. And each emptied jar was washed and sterilised and almost immediately filled with some new wine-to-be. Without realising it, I had started a hobby.

I've never ceased to marvel since at the range of things which can be turned into wine, and at the unexpectedly pleasing colours and tastes they produce. There have been failures, of course, some of them obviously my fault, a few quite inexplicable to an amateur. But the hobby has given much interest and satisfaction, not to mention supplied me with a varied range of wines at minimal cost, and no tax to pay. I make more than it would be judicious to drink, so there is the added pleasure of giving bottles to friends (to *sell* any, even for charity, is illegal). I must admit to a sly satisfaction when serving one of my 'country' wines from a decanter and being asked by its drinkers where I bought such an excellent rosé. I always own up, but it says a lot for the attainable results of making wine from everyday materials.

And it's that term – everyday materials – which gave me the idea and title for this book. When you come to consider it, you can literally drink your garden. If you like wine, and are prepared to go to the small effort and expense of making your own, that realisation will cause you henceforth to cast a new and thirsty look upon almost everything you grow. Fruits, berries, flowers, vegetables, leaves, even some weeds – all can be transformed into wines of delightful colour and interesting taste.

A sizeable, multi-purpose garden can make you self-sufficient: you might even find yourself planting new things especially to be made into wine, and that in itself could add a dimension to your interest in gardening. If you have only the merest patch it will still yield something, and for further supplies you can drink other people's gardens, or use the greengrocer as a sort of off-licence for materials.

Speaking of the greengrocer, I haven't hesitated to include in the recipes I offer some things which not many domestic gardeners produce. And, taking the view that a farm is a sort of extended garden, I have put in some of the brews which call for the use of barley, wheat, hops, and so forth.

The ingredients I've included are indigenous to both the UK and USA, hence there's an occasional doubling of names.

I am not a connoisseur or one of those experts who goes about judging home wine contests. I don't belong to a society or club, nor do I enter my produce in competitions; although for anyone who wishes to do those things there is much additional interest, pleasure and companionship to be gained.

The deeper scientific explanations of the wine-making process, with their terminology and tables of figures, I leave to others.

No, I'm simply someone who one day opened her door upon some parsnips – and drank them.

GLOSSARY

Air-lock Also called a fermentation lock, fermentation trap, air-trap, or 'bubbler'. A device used together with a bung to make the fermenting jar airtight.

Blending Mixing together different wines to correct over-sweetness, blandness, thinness, etc.

Body The wine's fullness, or substance.

Bouquet The wine's smell, or 'nose'.

Camden tablet A handy form of sulphur dioxide for disinfecting and sterilising.

Clearing The process by which cloudy material sinks to the bottom of the fermenting jar, leaving the wine crystal clear.

Dry Describes a wine free from all sweetness.

Fermentation The process by which yeast converts a sugared liquid into alcohol and carbon dioxide.

Fermenting jar Large glass vessel used for the secondary fermentation of wine.

Lees The sediment of dead yeast cells and other solids which collects at the bottom of the fermenting jar.

Maturing Storing wine in corked bottles to allow its body and bouquet to develop fully.

Must The pulp, the mixture of ingredients from which wine is made.

Racking Using a tube to siphon wine off the lees, to transfer it from one jar to another to help it clear.

Straining Passing the raw wine through finely meshed cloth to separate the liquid from solids suspended in it.

JOHN A. SALZER SEED CO'S ESTABLISHMENT, LA CROSSE, WIS.

JOHN A. SALZER
SEED CO.
LA CROSSE, WIS.

Spring
1899

EQUIPMENT

Home wine-making is one of the least expensive hobbies. You don't need to spend much on special equipment – in fact, apart from corks, air-locks and the like which can be bought very reasonably from any wine equipment supplier (listed in the telephone directory Yellow Pages – but if there isn't one near you, search the internet: most homebrew specialists trade online these days), most of the things you'll need are probably already in your kitchen. But please don't use chipped or cracked utensils, and make sure that any plastic vessels you use are food-grade. Wine-making is really no different from preparing food, and needs just the same amount of care in hygiene – clean hands, clean tools, and clean work surfaces.

For 1 gallon (4.5 l) of wine you'll need:

a boiling vessel a saucepan, or a preserving pan or fish-kettle, of at least 1½ gallon (6.75 l) capacity, to heat water and boil ingredients. It can be of stainless steel, good quality aluminium, sound enamel, even non-stick. Avoid using brass, iron or copper vessels, which will taint the wine.

a steeping vessel a large polythene bucket or other strong food-grade plastic container, to soak ingredients before fermentation.

a fermenting vessel a polythene bin or bucket, preferably with lid, is ideal for the primary, open fermentation. (You could use the same vessel for both steeping and fermenting.)

a fermenting jar 1 gallon (4.5 l) capacity, either glass or plastic. Demijohns with 'ear' handles are the easiest to manage and can be bought inexpensively from any wine equipment supplier. Dark glass is best for red wines, as it prevents them losing their colour.

kitchen scales for weighing ingredients.

a fruit press also called a wine press. The most expensive piece of equipment and only a necessity if you are making large quantities of wine, or if you are making cider. Soft fruits need to be lightly bruised to break the skins before pressing.

a mincer for dried fruit; also, if you don't have a fruit press, for hard-to-squeeze fruits such as apples.

a measuring jug for measuring liquids; also for measuring ingredients such as flower blossoms which are difficult to weigh.

a colander for washing dust and insects from freshly gathered blossom.

a lemon squeezer for extracting the juice from citrus fruit.

a plastic funnel for straining and bottling purposes.

a wooden mallet for crushing ingredients; or you could use the blunt end of a rolling pin, or the flat base of a bottle.

a wooden spoon for stirring purposes. Do avoid using metal spoons.

a siphon hose a length of plastic or rubber tubing, about 4 ft (1.2 m) long, for siphoning the wine from one container to another. Large vessels often come with outlet taps, but the standard 4.5l demijohn doesn't, and can only be emptied by siphoning.

a siphon stick a rigid tube with a filter at one end, essential to make sure you don't disturb the lees while siphoning.

straining cloths closely meshed nylon or muslin, or several thicknesses of cheesecloth. Never use a metal strainer.

a bottle brush for cleaning inside fermenting jars and wine bottles.

wine bottles any colour or shape, so long as they are *wine* bottles. Never use bottles intended for soft drinks, spirits or sauce. You can buy new wine bottles from equipment suppliers; but any licensed restaurant or similar premises will have plenty of empties to give away for re-use, if you ask.

bottle corks the straight-sided type. Use new ones every time – old corks are a source of infection and often not air-tight. Plastic 'corks' or stoppers are easier to use, but not as efficient.

bored bungs for use during the secondary, closed fermentation. You can buy cork bungs, but rubber ones are re-usable and less porous.

air-locks or fermentation traps, for use with the bungs. There are several types to choose from, both glass and plastic.

corking tool a simple device for inserting corks neatly and cleanly into wine bottle necks.

bottle labels for identifying your wines. They can be as simple or elaborate as you like.

cellar book a log book for keeping a record of each wine – the date started, variety of yeast, first racking, bottling, etc.

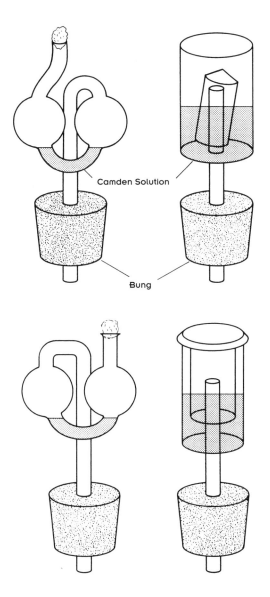

Camden Solution

Bung

Different types of air-lock, showing the correct levels of Camden solution in each

INGREDIENTS AND ADDITIVES

Main ingredient This is what gives the wine its individual colour, taste and smell, and the variety includes fruit, vegetables, flower blossom and herbs. They should not be used in quantities greater than 6 lbs per gallon of water (2.7 kg:4.5 l). Many of these ingredients can be re-used once they've played their part in the wine-making process: vegetables for stews and casseroles, fruit for jam and pie-fillings, tomatoes for chutney, dried fruit for curries.

Yeast This is the most vital ingredient in wine-making, its job being to convert sugar and oxygen into alcohol and carbon dioxide. There are several kinds of yeast available, and it's most important to use the right one, which is wine yeast. Baking yeast is for bread-making, and if you try making wine with it you'll end up with something that tastes strongly of baking yeast and little else. Brewing yeast is for making beer – use it for wine and the result will be cloudy and low in alcohol.

Wine yeast, developed by the commercial wine trade, is the only kind that will give you satisfactory results. It comes in powder, liquid or tablet form, and because it takes a little time to begin working, needs to be 'started' before adding to the must. This simply involves mixing a small amount of yeast with tepid water and a little sugar, covering and leaving in a warm place for a few hours. You'll find instructions on the container.

Wine yeast comes in a variety of types. A general purpose one is the most widely used, and is satisfactory for the beginner or part-time wine-maker. If you decide to go deeper into the hobby and want to experiment with some of the other varieties, they include:

for dry white wines	Hock or Chablis type yeasts
for sweet white wines	Sauternes or Tokay type yeasts
for red wines	Pommard, Burgundy or Bordeaux type yeasts
for heavy red wines	Port type yeasts

There are also special cereal yeasts for making wine from cereal crops; and a mead yeast for making wine from honey.

Yeast is a living organism, and like any other life form it needs the right conditions in order to thrive and work at its best. These conditions are warmth, oxygen, sugar, and nourishment which includes vitamins and minerals.

Yeast nutrient This is essential for the well-being of the yeast and must always be added with it. The nutrient contains the necessary vitamins and minerals, and it comes together with simple instructions for use in powder, tablet or liquid form. Without it the yeast can't do its job properly, and the wine suffers accordingly.

Sugar Only grapes contain enough natural sugar to make a good, strong wine. All other fruits and vegetables and blossom need extra sugar. Granulated white sugar is the most widely used because it doesn't affect the flavour or colour of the wine. Brown, or Demerara sugar can be used instead to give an insipid-looking wine an attractive golden colour, but it should never be used with delicately flavoured wines because its own flavour will submerge theirs.

Be careful to measure the exact amount of sugar for each recipe – too little results in a low alcohol content, too much produces a sickly sweet wine. The general rule is:

for a dry wine   2½ lbs (2 lbs US; 1.2 kg)
for a medium wine   3 lbs (2½ lbs US; 1.4 kg)
for a sweet wine   3½ lbs (3 lbs US; 1.6 kg)

It's always best to make your wine a little on the dry side – if it turns out too dry for your taste it can always be sweetened, but an already over-sweet wine can't be remedied except by blending. Sugar is generally added to the must in the form of syrup (ie. dissolved in hot water). This ensures that there are no undissolved sugar grains to affect the fermentation.

Pectin enzyme Pectin, or pectic acid, is found in stone fruits such as apricots, damsons and plums. It's a great aid in making jam, but a great hindrance in making wine. The acid is released from fruits and some vegetables during the initial soaking process, and must be destroyed or the wine will be cloudy. For this purpose, a pectin-destroying enzyme is introduced at the start of the wine-making programme. Note that it should only be added to cool, unsweetened pulp, since heat kills it and sugar prevents it from working properly. Pectin enzyme can be bought from any wine equipment supplier and comes under various brand names, including pectolase, pectozyme and pectinol. The amount to be used may vary from brand to brand, so read the container label directions carefully.

Grape tannin Most fruits contain some tannin (tannic acid), but not in sufficient quantity for wine-making purposes. Tannin is an important ingredient for several reasons: it helps prevent the wine from deteriorating, it adds body to the wine, and it enhances the flavour. Very little is needed – no more than half a teaspoon per gallon (4.5 l). Because tea is high in tannic acid some people prefer to use half a pint (284 ml) of strong cold black tea instead of powdered tannin. But I've found it affects the flavour and colour of the wine to some extent.

Camden tablets Indispensable for wine-making, these are a convenient source of sulphur dioxide and are used for disinfection. They sterilise equipment, preventing mould from growing on the must and bacteria from flourishing in the bottled wine. They will also kill any wild yeasts present in pulp or juice.

Camden tablets are easy and economical to use – one to each gallon (4.5 l) of wine is generally sufficient. Note that they should be added, crushed, at the start of the wine-making programme, since they will inhibit the working of the yeast if introduced at the fermentation stage. The air-locks used during the secondary fermentation should contain a Camden solution to prevent bacteria as well as oxygen from entering the fermenting jar; and a crushed tablet added to each gallon (4.5 l) of wine just before bottling will keep it free from contamination and bitterness and will help to preserve the colour.

A sterilising solution made from one Camden tablet to 4 ozs (114 ml) of water can be stored and re-used several times.

Make sure you never run out of them – there is no satisfactory substitute available on the high street. And don't be afraid to buy them in bulk – they have a shelf-life of 20 years!

Citric acid The less acid there is naturally present in the main ingredient, the more there is needed to be added. It helps the yeast to work, gives the wine 'bite' and helps to stabilise it, and prevents any medicinal flavours from creeping in. Citric acid is available in chemical form, but this tends to be expensive, and it's much easier (and nicer) to add it in the form of citrus fruit juice – lemon, orange or grapefruit. The amount of juice depends on the individual wine, but a general rule is between ½ oz and ¾ oz per gallon (14–21 ml:4.5 l).

Raisins and sultanas Dried fruit such as raisins and sultanas (called white raisins in the USA) are used to give body to an otherwise 'thin' wine, and add to its vinosity. They are also natural sweeteners, and 1 lb (453 g) of dried fruit is equal to ½s lb (226 g) of sugar. Because raisins have a flavour of their own, they shouldn't be used with blossom or other delicately flavoured wines or they will spoil the bouquet. For these, sultanas are best, being virtually flavourless. Dried fruit is prepared for use by chopping finely, or mincing.

Pearl barley Cereals such as pearl barley can be used with, or in place of, dried fruit with some wines, particularly those made from root vegetables, and have the same enhancing effect.

Root ginger Also called ginger root. This is another extra sometimes added to give wine a certain 'bite', and is prepared for use by bruising, or crushing slightly, to release the flavour. Most greengrocers and supermarkets stock it.

METHOD

Washing Like any other foodstuff, the ingredients must be fit to eat (or, in this case, drink), so reject anything that's unripe, mouldy or decaying. The skins are generally left on fruit and vegetables, so it's necessary to wash or scrub them thoroughly to remove all traces of dirt. Flower blossoms are put in a colander and rinsed under cold running water to wash away any dust and insects. Fruit such as blackberries need to be soaked in cold water for a short time to float out any maggots that might be in them.

Crushing or cutting At the start of the wine-making programme ingredients are crushed or cut to release their juice and colour. Soft fruits can be crushed with the hands, with a wooden mallet, the blunt end of a rolling pin, or even the base of a glass bottle. Stone fruits such as plums need a little extra care because it's important that the stones are not broken – if they are, they leave a most unpleasant taste in the wine. Hard fruits such as apples need to be finely chopped up and crushed in a fruit press. This type of fruit can be put through a kitchen mincer before pressing providing you take care to catch all the pulp and juice that runs out. Vegetables are cut up; except for runner bean pods, which must be broken by hand or too much unwanted starch will be released.

Boiling Some ingredients are boiled in order to yield their colour and flavour. Always cover the boiling vessel with a lid to prevent steam from escaping, and never over-cook the ingredients or the wine will be spoiled by cloudiness. They should be just tender, as though you were cooking them *al dente* and – needless to say – you do not add salt.

Soaking Many ingredients are covered with water after they've been crushed and left to steep or infuse for a period up to 48 hours. This allows the water to draw out the colour, flavour and aroma which will characterise the finished wine. A crushed Camden tablet and the pectin enzyme are added at this stage.

Mixing This is the point at which all the ingredients and additives come together in the fermenting vessel to make up the must. When adding the yeast, it's vital that the temperature is right for it – too much heat will kill it, too much cold will slow it right down. Test the liquid with a thermometer, and add the yeast when the reading is no higher than 80°F (27°C).

First, or primary fermentation As soon as the yeast starts to work, it gives off bubbles of carbon dioxide which cause the must to froth vigorously and turn a soupy colour. This on-the-must fermentation needs oxygen, so stir it well with a wooden spoon twice a day to air it and prevent the bottom layer from settling. Temperature plays an important part in the success of this primary stage. The fermenting vessel should be kept in a constant warmth of between 65°–75°F (18°–24°C), and you'll probably find that your kitchen, or even an airing cupboard, will do. If the temperature is higher than this, the wine will be bitter; at 95°F (35°C) or over, the yeast is killed.

During this vigorous frothing stage the must gives off a distinctive, pleasant aroma. It is attractive not only to the wine-maker but also to his deadliest enemy – the vinegar fly. This tiny insect seems to appear out of thin air and feeds on any fermenting substance, introducing bacteria which cause it to turn to vinegar ('sour wine', from the French *vinaigre*), so it must obviously not be allowed access. Except when the must is being stirred, the fermenting vessel should be kept well covered at all times, with a lid, or a large cloth or towel weighted with a board, or with a piece of securely held sheet plastic.

Straining After a few days the first vigorous fermentation begins to quieten as the yeast growth slows. The must is now ready to be strained into the fermenting jar. Twenty-four hours before you're ready to do this, fill the jar to the neck with Camden solution and likewise soak the bung and air-lock in solution. This sterilises your equipment. When you come to empty the jar there's no need to dry inside – what little moisture is left is beneficial.

Cover the table top or whatever surface you're using with newspaper, to catch any drips. Insert a plastic funnel into the neck of the fermenting jar and over this spread a straining cloth. Using a plastic jug, pour the liquid carefully through the cloth and into the jar. It's important not to rush this stage or you may well have trouble clearing the wine later on. The fermenting jar should be filled just to where the shoulder meets the neck. Keep any left-over liquid in a covered container – you'll need it to top up the jar if the ferment froths up through the air-lock.

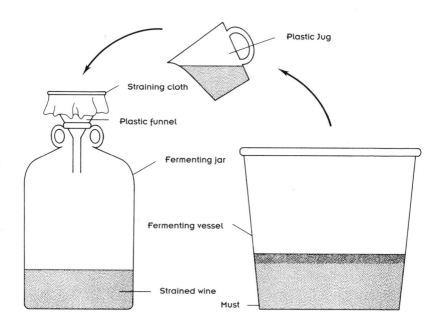

Straining the raw wine into a fermenting jar at the end of the primary fermentation

Secondary fermentation The wine is now ready for the secondary, or closed fermentation and will be a curious milky or muddy colour. Fermenting conditions are reversed: the young wine must be denied oxygen, forcing the yeast to use other means of survival and thereby producing even more alcohol; and it must be left undisturbed to allow dead yeast cells and other debris to form a solid layer of sediment – called the lees – at the bottom of the jar. If the jar is constantly being moved at this stage, this sediment will remain suspended in the wine and prevent it clearing.

In order to stop oxygen reaching the yeast, the fermenting jar must be closed off with a bung and an air-lock – a simple valve which allows the carbon dioxide gas given off by the yeast to escape, but prevents air (and bacteria) from entering. The air-lock is half-filled with Camden solution, the tube at its base is inserted firmly into the central hole of the bung, and the bung in turn is inserted firmly into the neck of the fermenting jar. Some people prefer to fit the air-lock *after* the bung has gone into the jar, but I find this often causes particles of cork, and especially rubber, to be scraped off into the wine below.

Label the jar clearly with the name of the wine, using a tie-on label, a strip of Dymo tape, or whatever's convenient.

The young wine is now left alone to continue its fermentation, and it does this best if stored in a draught-free place with a constant temperature of around 60°F (15°C). Within a short time of the air-lock being fitted bubbles will begin to escape, making that distinctive 'plop' which is one of the attractions of wine-making. Not only is it a pleasant, almost musical sound, but there's the added satisfaction of knowing that for every bubble released your wine has gained an equal weight of alcohol.

At first the bubbling will be fairly rapid, but after a while it begins to quieten. As the amount of alcohol in the wine increases, the number of live yeast cells dwindles and the bubbles grow fewer. After a few weeks or so – the time varies according to the individual wine – a thick sediment will have formed on the floor of the jar and the wine will start to clear from the top downwards. Now is the time to rack it.

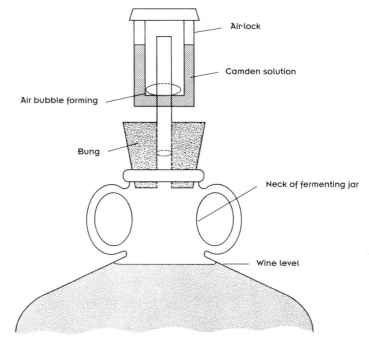

Air-lock

Camden solution

Air bubble forming

Bung

Neck of fermenting jar

Wine level

Air-lock and bung fitted into the neck of the fermenting jar for the secondary, without air-fermentation

Racking Though the hobby does at times call for a little stretching of limbs and racking of brains, the expression 'racking' as used in wine-making is derived from the Provençal *raca*, meaning 'dregs', and describes the method by which young wine is siphoned off the lees to help it clear and stop it picking up any 'off' flavours. Twenty-four hours before you intend racking your wine, sterilise a clean fermenting jar, bung and air-lock with Camden solution, as I've already described, this time including a length of siphon tubing.

When you come to rack, move the jar containing the wine to a steady surface, such as a table top (try not to disturb the contents more than you can help) and place the clean empty jar close to it, at a lower level – on a chair or stool. Now remove the air-lock and insert the

Drink Your Own Garden

siphon stick through the bung. Its filter or foot should rest lightly on the bottom of the jar. Attach the siphon tube to the protruding end of the siphon stick. Put the other end of the tubing into your mouth, suck hard and immediately transfer that end to the new jar. The wine will be drawn by atmospheric pressure out of the full jar and along the tubing. You may find that the new fermenting jar isn't quite full to the base of the neck, and needs topping up. It's important to do this, because too much air space inside the jar encourages deterioration of the wine. You can either use a previously made wine of the same variety, or any surplus juice from when you originally pressed the fruit (it freezes well!), or a syrup made of 8 ozs of sugar to 5 ozs of water (226 g:142 ml), first boiled until dissolved, then added when cool. Topping up with plain water isn't a good idea because it dilutes the wine and lowers the alcohol content.

Fit the new jar with bung and air-lock and leave the wine to continue its quiet fermentation. If another thick sediment forms after a time, rack again –too much racking is better for the wine than standing on a thick, ill-flavoured sediment.

When you wash out the fermenting jar, don't throw this sediment away – it makes excellent plant fertilizer! And don't forget to store washed jars with a little Camden solution inside each, to discourage mould growth.

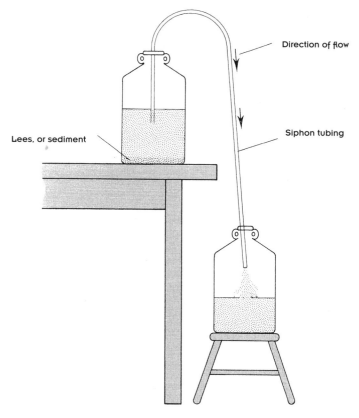

Racking the young wine into a clean fermenting jar

Clearing This is also called clarification, and is the process by which the wine gradually loses its original soupy appearance and becomes a crystal clear liquid. It's a slow business, and needs patience and time to complete. However, if your wine is still cloudy after 9 months or so, turn to the section on Remedies (p29) to get things moving.

As the wine grows clearer the fermentation grows slower, and eventually ceases altogether. Once it has finished and the wine has

Drink Your Own Garden

The image contains the labels:

Direction of flow

Lees, or sediment

Siphon tubing

cleared completely, it's time to do the bottling. But – caution! – double check first to ensure that fermentation *has* quite finished. It can sometimes start up again, and if you've bottled prematurely you risk blown corks, burst bottles and wasted wine. A good test is to move the jar into a slightly higher temperature for a week or so, and watch to see whether any bubbles appear in the air-lock. If so, wait a while longer; if not, go ahead and bottle your wine.

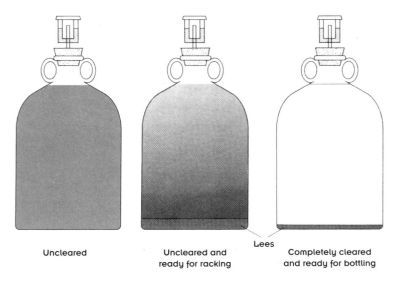

Uncleared   **Uncleared and**   Lees   **Completely cleared**
          ready for racking   **and ready for bottling**

Three stages in the clearing of the young wine

Bottling NB. Use *wine* bottles only – they're the only type that can withstand pressure (apart from beer bottles which you probably wouldn't use for wine anyway) and to use any other kind, whether screw-top or spirit, is asking for trouble. Serious injury can be caused by bottles bursting suddenly and spraying glass about.

One imperial gallon of wine (4.5 l) will fill 6½ standard wine bottles. If you're using second-hand bottles, soak them first in warm water to remove the labels, then wash them thoroughly, using a bottle brush to clean inside. Twenty-four hours before you bottle your wine, fill each bottle with Camden solution to disinfect and sterilise it – there's no need to dry inside when you come to tip the solution out. Count out the number of wine corks you'll need, plus a couple extra in case of mishaps, and soak them in Camden solution in a bowl or basin, pressing them down with a plate to keep them submerged. This both sterilises and softens the corks, making them easier to insert. If you prefer to use plastic 'corks' they'll need to be sterilised too.

Probably the easiest way to fill each bottle is to use the siphon tubing and a plastic jug for topping up. Set the fermenting jar at a higher level than the bottle, and move the tubing from one to another as each is filled. I find it convenient to stand the bottles in a washing-up bowl – it keeps them together and catches any spills. Too much air left inside will encourage vinegar bacteria to flourish, so fill each bottle to within ½ inch (13 mm) of the cork bottom (to estimate this, hold the cork outside the bottle neck so that both tops are flush).

Now insert the corks, using a corker or corking machine (much the easiest method) or a 'flogger' (a short flat piece of wood) and mallet, and drive each cork in so that it's just flush with the bottle neck opening. If you're using plastic stoppers, simply push them in by hand. Some wine-makers like to cover the cork with a metal foil or plastic capsule, available from wine equipment suppliers, to protect it against possible damage by cork moth during the storage period.

Finally, the bottles are labelled with the name of the wine, the date it was begun (its vintage date) and the date of bottling. Blank gummed labels can be bought cheaply for this purpose; but if you want to be more imaginative you can design your own personalised labels and have them printed.

Storing Ideally, wine should be stored in a place that is cool, dark and free from vibration. Light frequently spoils bottled wine, robbing it of its colour and flavour, and too high a temperature will affect it badly too. The best storage place is, of course, a cellar or basement, but a cool out-of-the-way cupboard will do, providing the temperature is constant at about 50°F (10°C). A garage or out-house are possibilities, as long as the bottles are stored well out of the way of fumes and strong-smelling materials. Attics tend to be unsuitable for storage because their temperature varies so much.

Stand the bottles upright for the first day or two, because pressure sometimes forces out a still-wet cork, and less wine is spilled from an upright bottle. After this short safety period the bottles are stored on their sides, label uppermost, in a wine or bottle rack or other suitable container. This ensures that the wine is kept in contact with the corks, preventing them from drying out and shrinking and so risking contamination and leaks.

During the storage period the wine matures and mellows, a process that takes at least 6 months (apart from flower wines which are ready after 4 months). It really is a waste to drink it before then, and unfair both to the wine and to yourself. Generally, white wines are ready to drink earlier than red wines.

Serving It's always a good idea to serve home-made wine in a decanter. Not only does it look very attractive, but decanting lets air into the wine and allows it to breathe, developing to the full its bouquet and flavour. An hour in the decanter before serving will bring out the best in your wine.

SUMMARY OF THE WINE-MAKING METHOD

1. Extract flavour and colour by crushing, soaking, and/or boiling.

2. Add sugar and other ingredients; add yeast when the must is just comfortably warm and ferment in a covered vessel at 65°–75°F (18°–24°C), stirring twice daily.

3. Strain into a fermenting jar, fit bung and air-lock and leave to ferment on undisturbed at about 60°F (15°C).

4. Rack when the wine begins to clear from the top, and a thick sediment has formed at the bottom. Repeat racking as further sediment builds up.

5. Bottle when the wine is completely clear and all fermentation has ceased.

6. Store in a cool, dark place for at least 6 months before drinking.

FAULTS AND REMEDIES

Home wine-making is a simple procedure requiring only a little care, common-sense and attention to produce gratifying results. The rules are few, but it is important to observe them to avoid spoilt wines.

Do gather well-ripened ingredients on a warm dry day to ensure maximum flavour and bouquet.

Do follow recipes carefully and completely.

Do keep equipment properly sterilized and working conditions hygienic.

Do observe correct temperatures for individual fermenting stages.

Do keep the first fermentation well covered, and the second fermentation away from air.

Do use wine bottles and new corks.

Don't include dirty, mouldy or badly damaged ingredients.

Don't use any metal equipment, other than the boiling vessel.

Don't use any kind of disinfectant or sterilising fluid other than Camden solution (sodium metabisulphite).

Don't let the wine stand too long on thick sediment – rack as often as necessary.

Don't leave too much air space between liquid and cork.

Don't rush – poor wine is often the result of a hurried process.

Of course, what suits one palate might not suit another, and it's up to the individual wine-maker to experiment and discover which variety of wines are personally pleasing, and which are not, and so plan his programme accordingly. It sometimes happens that even the best recipe in the most careful hands produces a wine which is rather less than perfect, but most faults can be remedied. The most common are:

Sticking ferment The yeast should begin to work within six hours of being added to the must at the start of the first fermenting stage. If it doesn't, this 'sticking' is probably due to one of the following:

a) Incorrect temperature. When the yeast is added, the temperature of the must should be around 77°F (25°C) (see page 19). If it's too hot the yeast is killed; if it's too cold the yeast growth is held back. Also check the temperature of the room where the fermenting vessel is kept during this first stage – it should be constant at between 65°–75°F (18°–24°C), day and night, with no draughts. If there's no sign at all of fermentation starting, make up a fresh batch of yeast and stir it into the must. Sticking in the secondary, without-air fermentation can likewise be caused by incorrect temperature, usually one that is too low. Try moving the jar to a warmer place.

b) Sulphur dioxide. Freshly added Camden tablets inhibit fermentation and should not be mixed with the must at the same time as the yeast. Always allow at least 24 hours for the dispersal of the sulphur dioxide in the tablets before introducing the yeast. If you *have* added the two together and suspect this is the reason for the ferment sticking, stir the must vigorously once an hour two or three times to disperse the gas, then let it settle overnight. If the yeast hasn't started fermenting by next morning it's obviously been destroyed. Make up a fresh batch of yeast and add to the must.

c) Lack of yeast nutrient. This is a vital ingredient, necessary to help the yeast to thrive. If you've forgotten to include it in the must, do so now: mix the correct amount of nutrient in a cup of tepid water and stir it in. Too much nutrient is better than none at all.

d) Lack of acid. Just occasionally insufficient acid is the cause of a sticking ferment. If the recipe calls for citric acid (lemon, orange or grapefruit juice), don't neglect to use it.

Failure to clear After 9 months in the fermenting jar, the wine should have cleared completely. If it's still cloudy after this time try moving the jar into a lower temperature – a cool larder or out-house – and leave it for another month or so. If the wine still refuses to clear naturally, you may have over-boiled the ingredients and released too much starch, or you may have hurried the straining process and allowed too much solid material to stay in the wine. The remedy is to use an artificial clearer, called a fining agent. A variety of brands are available from wine equipment suppliers, and are simple to use. The fining agent works within a day or two and carries the cloudy material to the bottom of the jar, leaving the clear wine to be siphoned off into a fresh jar. Alternatively, egg shells can be used in the same way to clear a white wine. The empty, cleaned shells are baked in a hot oven until they're brittle, then crushed finely and scattered on the wine surface. As the fragments rise and fall, they carry down any suspended solids.

Hazes Not to be confused with the cloudiness of an uncleared wine. A coloured haze (usually white, purplish or brown) means metal contamination, caused by using equipment made of iron, zinc, brass or copper. If the haze is only slight, it can be cleared by adding a small amount of citric acid. If the haze is pronounced, the wine is poisoned and MUST NOT BE DRUNK. Pour it down the drain – and take care next time to observe the general rule that no metal of any kind (apart from the initial boiling vessel) should be used in wine-making.

Acetification – or the formation of vinegar. This is the result of contamination by bacteria, and may happen if your equipment is not properly sterilised, or if the secondary fermentation has been exposed too much to air. The first signs are a vinegary smell and a slight acid taste to the wine. At this early stage the wine can still be saved by adding one crushed Camden tablet, leaving for 24 hours, then stirring in a fresh batch of yeast. If the contamination has spread too far, the smell of vinegar is very strong and so is the acid taste. There's no remedy at this late stage – your wine is vinegar. Use it for salad dressings or whatever, but don't drink it. Avoid future error by practising careful sterilisation, and by keeping the first ferment well covered, the second ferment tightly bunged, and your bottles filled to the correct level.

Flowers of wine A pretty expression for an ugly infection caused by airborne bacteria which gain access to the wine if too much air is allowed into the fermenting jar. Don't confuse them with the ring-mark sometimes left by the froth of a vigorous ferment. The first signs are powdery flecks like dandruff appearing on the wine surface. If they're left, they multiply rapidly and reverse the wine process, turning it back into carbon dioxide and water. In the early stages the wine can be treated with two crushed Camden tablets, then filtered carefully through filter paper or unmedicated cotton wool into a freshly sterilised jar and a fresh batch of yeast added. If the infection isn't detected until the later stages, when a white skin completely covers the wine surface, it's too late to do anything – except pour it down the drain.

Ropiness – also called oiliness. Although its taste is unchanged, the wine appears thick and slimy, and pours very slowly. This is caused by lactic acid bacteria, and looks much worse than it really is. The condition is fairly easy to correct – add two crushed Camden tablets to the wine, stir it vigorously to break up the rope-like coils, then filter it into a clean jar through filter paper (available from wine equipment suppliers). Sometimes the ropiness is due to too much sugar syrup remaining suspended in the wine. Rack it into a clean jar, holding the siphon tube fairly high up in the bottle neck so that the wine splashes down, allowing it to be aired and thoroughly shaken up at the same time.

Poor wine A disappointing wine may be due to flatness, or insipidity; over-sweetness; thinness, or lack of body. Flatness is the result of too little grape tannin in the wine and can be remedied by stirring in a small amount and leaving for a while. Over-sweetness is caused by using too much sugar, and neglecting to use a yeast nutrient. Try adding a small amount of citric acid or lemon juice, then air the wine by pouring it quickly from one jar to another and back again. Thinness is due to an insufficient amount of the basic ingredient, especially in the case of a fruit wine. Both thinness and over-sweetness can be remedied by blending the poor wine with a dry, full-bodied one of the same ingredient-type, or with a good dry low-flavoured wine such as rhubarb.

Off flavours A musty-flavoured wine is usually the result of letting it stand too long on the sediment, or lees. Next time, observe the general rule – once a firm sediment has formed, rack the wine.

SEASONAL CALENDAR OF WINES

Late winter – early spring

Beetroot	Clementine	Birch sap
Carrot	Grapefruit	Sycamore sap
Parsnip	Lemon	Walnut sap
Potato	Lime	
Turnip	Orange	

Late spring – early summer

Broad bean	Cherry	Broom (gorse)	Balm
Lettuce	Gooseberry	Clover	Bramble tip
Lima bean	Raspberry	Coltsfoot	Mint
Pea pod	Rhubarb	Cowslip	Nettle
Spinach	Strawberry	Dandelion	Parsley
		Elderflower	Thyme
		Golden rod	
		Hawthorn (may)	
		Honeysuckle	
		Lime blossom	
		Marigold	Oak leaf
		Primrose	Walnut leaf

Late summer – early autumn

Aubergine (eggplant)	Apple	Bilberry	Carnation
Marrow (squash)	Apricot	Blackberry	Rose
Melon	Banana	Blueberry	
Pumpkin	Bullace	Cloudberry	
Runner bean	Damson	Cranberry	
Tomato	Fig	Currants	
	Grape	Dewberry	Hop
	Greengage	Elderberry	
	Nectarine	Folly	
	Peach	Loganberry	
	Pear	Mulberry	
	Plum	Wineberry	
			Mead

Late autumn – early winter

Artichoke (sun choke)	Crab apple	Hawthornberry	Oak leaf
Celery	Medlar	Rosehip	Walnut leaf
Mangold (sugar beet)	Quince	Rowanberry	
		Sloe	Barley
			Maize
			Rice
			Rye
			Wheat

NOTE ON MEASURES

The measures used in this book are Imperial (British), US and Metric, and are given individually for each recipe. I have taken into account the difference between the Imperial and US pint by adjusting the amounts of ingredients for each wine.

Weight

1 oz = 28.3 grammes

1 lb = 453.6 grammes

1 gramme = 0.035 oz

1 kilogramme = 2.2 lbs

Volume

1 imp. pint = 1.25 US pints

1 imp. pint = 568 ml

1 US pint = 16 imp. fl. ozs

1 US pint = 473 ml

Temperature

Fahrenheit	Centigrade
50	10
59	15
68	20
77	25
86	30
95	35

RECIPES

BERRY
& BUSH
WINES

BILBERRY

Bilberries – also known as blaeberries, whinberries and whortleberries – make a good dry red wine, but avoid using too many or the flavour will be unpleasantly strong.

	IMP	US	METRIC
ripe bilberries	2 lbs	1¾ lbs	905 g
sugar	2½ lbs	2 lbs	1.2 kg
lemon	1	1	1
Camden tablets	2	2	2
pectin enzyme	1 tsp	1 tsp	1 tsp
water	1 gallon	1 gallon	4.5 l
wine yeast			
yeast nutrient			

1. Put the washed fruit into the fermenting vessel, crush well and cover with 6 pints (3.4 l) of boiling water.
2. When cool, add the crushed Camden tablets and pectin enzyme and leave to steep for 24 hours.
3. Bring a further 2 pints (1.1 l) of water to the boil and dissolve the sugar in it. Cool to blood heat and add to the bilberry pulp together with the yeast and nutrient and the juice of the lemon.
4. Cover the vessel and leave to ferment in a warm place for 4 days, stirring twice daily.
5. Strain the liquid off the pulp and transfer to a fermenting jar. Close off with an air-lock and leave to ferment on, racking when the wine begins to clear.
6. When all fermentation has ceased and the wine cleared completely, bottle and store in a cool dark place to mature for at least 6 months, preferably 9 months.

BLACKBERRY (OR BRAMBLE)

Ripe, juicy blackberries gathered on a sunny day make a delicious deep red wine. It's best to ferment this in a dark glass jar to prevent light spoiling the colour. Don't be tempted to exceed the given quantity of fruit or the wine will be too astringent. This recipe can also be used to make cloudberry, dewberry and wineberry wines.

	IMP	US	METRIC
ripe blackberries	4 lbs	3¼ lbs	1.8 kg
sugar	3 lbs	2½ lbs	1.4 kg
lemon	1	1	1
Camden tablet	1	1	1
pectin enzyme	1 tsp	1 tsp	1 tsp
water	1 gallon	1 gallon	4.5 l
wine yeast			
yeast nutrient			

1. Wash the blackberries thoroughly to remove any maggots. Put into the fermenting vessel, crush well and cover with 6 pints (3.4 l) of boiling water. When cool, add the crushed Camden tablet and pectin enzyme and leave to steep for 24 hours.
2. Bring a further 2 pints (1.1 l) of water to the boil and dissolve the sugar in it. Cool to blood heat and add to the blackberry pulp together with the yeast and nutrient and the juice of the lemon.
3. Cover the vessel and leave to ferment in a warm place for 3 days, stirring twice daily.
4. Strain the liquid off the pulp and transfer to a fermenting jar. Close off with an air-lock and leave to ferment on, racking when the wine starts to clear.

5. When all fermentation has ceased and the wine cleared, bottle and store in a cool dark place to mature for at least 6 months.

6. For variations using other autumn fruits – not exceeding 6 lbs (5 lbs US; 2.7 kg) of mixed fruit to 1 gallon (4.5 l) of water – use this recipe to make Blackberry & Apple; Blackberry & Elderberry; Blackberry & Rosehip; and Blackberry & Sloe.

BLUEBERRY

The blueberry is the North American cousin of the British bilberry. It's a sweet fruit, characteristically blue, sometimes black, when ripe, and unlike the single-fruited bilberry it grows in many-fruited clusters.

	IMP	US	METRIC
ripe blueberries	2 lbs	1¾ lbs	905 g
sugar	2 lbs	1¾ lbs	905 g
sultanas	1 lb	14 ozs	453 g
lemon	1	1	1
Camden tablet	1	1	1
pectin enzyme	1 tsp	1 tsp	1 tsp
water	1 gallon	1 gallon	4.5 l
wine yeast			
yeast nutrient			

1. Put the washed fruit into the fermenting vessel, crush well and cover with 6 pints (3.4 l) of boiling water.
2. When cool, stir in the crushed Camden tablet and pectin enzyme and leave to steep for 24 hours.
3. Bring a further 2 pints (1.1 l) of water to the boil and dissolve the sugar in it.
4. Cool this syrup to blood heat, then add to the fruit pulp together with the yeast and nutrient, the sultanas and lemon juice.
5. Cover the vessel and leave in a warm place to ferment for 5–6 days, stirring twice daily.
6. Strain the liquid off the pulp and transfer to a fermenting jar. Close off with an air-lock and leave to ferment on, racking when the wine begins to clear.
7. When all fermentation has ceased and the wine is completely clear, bottle and store in a cool dark place to mature for at least 9 months, preferably a year.

BRAMBLE TIP

Brambles are the thorny bushes on which blackberries grow, and the tips are picked when they're young and succulent, about 5 inches (13 cm) long. They're awkward to weigh, so use a kitchen jug to measure them, packing them down reasonably tightly.

	IMP	US	METRIC
bramble tips	1 gallon	1 gallon	4.5 l
sugar	3 lbs	2½ lbs	1.4 kg
lemons	2	2	2
orange	1	1	1
Camden tablet	1	1	1
water	1 gallon	1 gallon	4.5 l
wine yeast			
yeast nutrient			

1. Crush the Camden tablet in a gallon (4.5 l) of cold water and soak the bramble tips in this overnight.
2. Bring water and tips to the boil and simmer gently for 15 minutes. Strain the water on to the sugar and dissolve thoroughly.
3. Leave until comfortably warm before adding the yeast and nutrient and citrus fruit juice.
4. Cover and leave in a warm place to ferment for 5 days, stirring twice daily. Transfer to a fermenting jar, fit an air-lock and leave to ferment on, racking when the wine starts to clear.
5. Once all fermentation has ceased, bottle and store in a cool dark place to mature for at least 6 months.

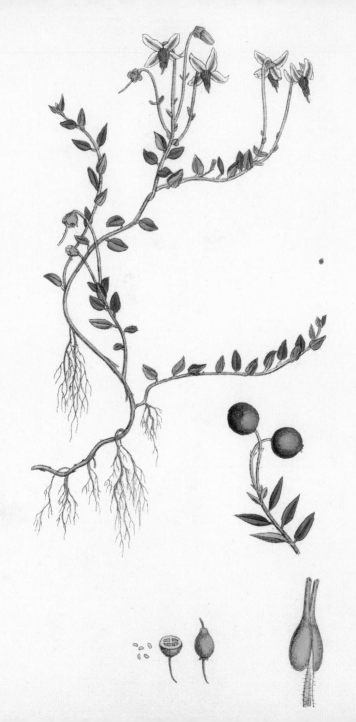

CRANBERRY

The small red cranberry is one of the less outstanding country wines, but probably worth making if you have a glut of fruit.

	IMP	US	METRIC
ripe cranberries	4 lbs	3¼ lbs	1.8 kg
sugar	3 lbs	2½ lbs	1.4 kg
raisins	8 ozs	7 ozs	226 g
Camden tablet	1	1	1
pectin enzyme	1 tsp	1 tsp	1 tsp
water	7 pints	7 pints	4 l
wine yeast			
yeast nutrient			

1. Put the washed cranberries into the fermenting vessel, crush well and cover with 5 pints (2.8 l) of boiling water.
2. When cool, stir in the crushed Camden tablet and pectin enzyme and leave to steep for 48 hours.
3. Bring a further 2 pints (1.1 l) of water to the boil and dissolve the sugar in it.
4. Add this syrup to the cranberry pulp, then stir in the yeast, nutrient and raisins.
5. Cover and leave in a warm place to ferment for 4 days, stirring twice daily. Strain the liquid off the pulp, measure and if necessary make up to 1 gallon (4.5 l) with cool boiled water.
6. Transfer to a fermenting jar, fit an air-lock and leave to ferment on, racking when the wine is beginning to clear.
7. When all fermentation has ceased and the wine is completely clear, bottle and store in a cool dark place to mature for at least 6 months.

BLACK CURRANT

There are three varieties of currant – black, red and white – and the method of wine-making is the same for each. Black currants have the strongest flavour and produce a good sweet wine.

	IMP	US	METRIC
ripe black currants	3 lbs	2½ lbs	1.4 kg
sugar	3 lbs	2½ lbs	1.4 kg
Camden tablet	1	1	1
pectin enzyme	1 tsp	1 tsp	1 tsp
water	7 pints	7 pints	4 l
wine yeast			
yeast nutrient			

1. Put the washed currants into the fermenting vessel, crush well and cover with 5 pints (2.8 l) of boiling water.
2. When cool, stir in the crushed Camden tablet and pectin enzyme and leave to steep for 24 hours.
3. Bring a further 2 pints (1.1 l) of water to the boil and dissolve the sugar in it.
4. Stir this syrup into the currant pulp, then add the yeast and nutrient.
5. Cover closely and leave to ferment in a warm place for 4–5 days, stirring twice daily.
6. Strain the liquid off the pulp, measure and if necessary make up to 1 gallon (4.5 l) with cool boiled water.
7. Transfer to a fermenting jar, close off with an air-lock and leave to ferment on, racking when the wine starts to clear.
8. When all fermentation has ceased and the wine cleared, bottle and store in a cool dark place to mature for at least 6 months. The black currant wine will be ready to drink a little earlier than the others.

RED CURRANT

Red and white currants are best when made drier. The easiest way to strip the berries from the stalks is to draw them through the prongs of an ordinary table fork.

	IMP	US	METRIC
ripe red currants	4 lbs	3¼ lbs	1.8 kg
sugar	2½ lbs	2 lbs	1.2 kg
lemon	1	1	1
Camden tablet	1	1	1
pectin enzyme	1 tsp	1 tsp	1 tsp
water	7 pints	7 pints	4 l
wine yeast			
yeast nutrient			

1. Put the washed currants into the fermenting vessel, crush well and cover with 5 pints (2.8 l) of boiling water.
2. When cool, stir in the crushed Camden tablet and pectin enzyme and leave to steep for 24 hours.
3. Bring a further 2 pints (1.1 l) of water to the boil and dissolve the sugar in it.
4. Stir this syrup into the currant pulp, then add the yeast and nutrient (and for red and white currants only, the juice of the lemon).
5. Cover closely and leave to ferment in a warm place for 4–5 days, stirring twice daily.
6. Strain the liquid off the pulp, measure and if necessary make up to 1 gallon (4.5 l) with cool boiled water.
7. Transfer to a fermenting jar, close off with an air-lock and leave to ferment on, racking when the wine starts to clear.
8. When all fermentation has ceased and the wine cleared, bottle and store in a cool dark place to mature for at least 6 months.

WHITE CURRANT

Red and white currants are best when made drier. The easiest way to strip the berries from the stalks is to draw them through the prongs of an ordinary table fork.

	IMP	US	METRIC
ripe white currants	4 lbs	3¼ lbs	1.8 kg
sugar	2½ lbs	2 lbs	1.2 kg
lemon	1	1	1
Camden tablet	1	1	1
pectin enzyme	1 tsp	1 tsp	1 tsp
water	7 pints	7 pints	4 l
wine yeast			
yeast nutrient			

Follow the recipe for Red currant (p.52)

For a mixed currant wine:

black currants	2 lbs	1¾ lbs	905 g
red currants	1 lb	14 ozs	453 g
white currants	1 lb	14 ozs	453 g

ELDERBERRY

Choose berries growing in large clusters on red stalks for a sweet, full-bodied red wine. They contain a lot of tannin, so don't exceed the given amount or the wine will be too astringent.

	IMP	US	METRIC
ripe elderberries	3½ lbs	3 lbs	1.6 kg
sugar	3 lbs	2½ lbs	1.4 kg
sultanas	1 lb	14 ozs	453 g
lemon	1	1	1
Camden tablet	1	1	1
pectin enzyme	½ tsp	½ tsp	½ tsp
water	7 pints	7 pints	4 l
wine yeast			
yeast nutrient			

1. Strip the berries from the stalks by drawing them through the prongs of a table fork. Wash them, put them into the fermenting vessel and crush well.
2. Cover with 5 pints (2.8 l) of cold water, stir in the crushed Camden tablet and pectin enzyme, and leave to steep for 2 days, stirring occasionally. Bring a further 2 pints (1.1 l) of water to the boil and dissolve the sugar in it.
3. Cool this syrup to blood heat and add it to the elderberry pulp, followed by the yeast and nutrient, the juice of the lemon and the minced sultanas. Cover the vessel and leave in a warm place to ferment for 3 days, stirring twice daily.
4. Strain the liquid off the pulp, measure and if necessary make up to 1 gallon (4.5 l) with cool boiled water.
5. Transfer to a fermenting jar, fit bung and air-lock and leave to ferment on, racking when the wine starts to clear.
6. When all fermentation has ceased, and the wine is completely clear, bottle and store in a cool dark place to mature for at least 6 months.

GOOSEBERRY

Gooseberries are versatile fruit for wine-making – the unripe green berries produce a crisp dry white wine, the ripe red berries a sweeter one.

GREEN GOOSEBERRY	IMP	US	METRIC
green gooseberries	3 lbs	2½ lbs	1.4 kg
sugar	2½ lbs	2 lbs	1.2 kg
Camden tablet	1	1	1
pectin enzyme	1 tsp	1 tsp	1 tsp
grape tannin	½ tsp	½ tsp	½ tsp
water	1 gallon	1 gallon	4.5 l
wine yeast			
yeast nutrient			

RED GOOSEBERRY			
red gooseberries	4 lbs	3¼lbs	1.8 kg
sugar	3 lbs	2½ lbs	1.4 kg
Camden tablet	1	1	1
pectin enzyme	1 tsp	1 tsp	1 tsp
grape tannin	½s tsp	½ tsp	½ tsp
water	1 gallon	1 gallon	4.5 l
wine yeast			
yeast nutrient			

1. Put the gooseberries into the fermenting vessel and crush thoroughly until they are pulpy.
2. Cover with 6 pints (3.4 l) of cold water, add the crushed Camden tablet and pectin enzyme and leave to steep for 48 hours, stirring occasionally. Heat a further 2 pints (1.1 l) of water to boiling point, dissolve the sugar in it, and when cool add to the gooseberry pulp.

3. Stir in the yeast, nutrient and grape tannin, cover well and leave to ferment in a warm place for 2–3 days.
4. Strain the liquid off the pulp and transfer to a fermenting jar. Close off with an air-lock and leave to ferment on, racking when the wine starts to clear.
5. When all fermentation has ceased and the wine has cleared, bottle and store in a cool dark place to mature for at least 1 year.

HAWTHORNBERRY

This is a pleasantly flavoured autumn wine made from the ripe red haws, or fruit, of the hawthorn bush.

	IMP	US	METRIC
ripe hawthorn berries	4 lbs	3¼ lbs	1.8 kg
sugar	3 lbs	2½ lbs	1.4 kg
sultanas	8 ozs	7 ozs	226 g
lemons	2	2	2
Camden tablet	1	1	1
pectin enzyme	1 tsp	1 tsp	1 tsp
water	1 gallon	1 gallon	4.5 l
wine yeast			
yeast nutrient			

1. Crush the berries well in the fermenting vessel and cover with 6 pints (3.4 l) of boiling water. Leave this to cool, then stir in the crushed Camden tablet and pectin enzyme. Cover and steep for 2 days, stirring occasionally. Bring a further 2 pints (1.1 l) of water to the boil and dissolve the sugar in it.

2. When this syrup has cooled to blood heat, add it to the pulp together with the yeast and nutrient, the juice of the lemons and the minced sultanas. Cover the vessel and leave in a warm place to ferment for 4 days, stirring twice daily.

3. Strain the juice off the pulp and transfer to a fermenting jar. Close off with an air-lock and leave to ferment on, racking when the wine starts to clear.

4. When all fermentation has ended and the wine is clear, bottle and store in a cool dark place to mature for at least 6 months.

LOGANBERRY

The loganberry is a hybrid fruit – a cross between a blackberry and a raspberry – and makes a very pleasant sweet wine.

	IMP	US	METRIC
ripe loganberries	3 lbs	2½ lbs	1.4 kg
sugar	3½ lbs	3 lbs	1.6 kg
Camden tablet	1	1	1
pectin enzyme	1 tsp	1 tsp	1 tsp
water	1 gallon	1 gallon	4.5 l
wine yeast			
yeast nutrient			

1. Put the washed loganberries into a vessel, crush thoroughly and cover with 6 pints (3.4 l) of cold water. Add the crushed Camden tablet and pectin enzyme and leave to steep for 24 hours.

2. Bring a further 2 pints (1.1 l) of water to the boil, dissolve the sugar in it, and when this syrup has cooled, add it to the loganberry pulp.

3. Stir in the yeast and nutrient, cover the vessel and leave in a warm place to ferment for 4 days, stirring twice daily.

4. Strain the liquid off the pulp and transfer to a fermenting jar. Fit an air-lock and leave to ferment on, racking when the wine starts to clear. When all fermentation has ceased and the wine has cleared, bottle and store in a cool dark place to mature for at least 6 months.

MULBERRY

Mulberries make a good sweet red wine which needs maturing well. Gather the berries when they're quite black and at their ripest.

	IMP	US	METRIC
ripe mulberries	4 lbs	3¼ lbs	1.8 kg
sugar	3½ lbs	3 lbs	1.6 kg
Camden tablet	1	1	1
pectin enzyme	1 tsp	1 tsp	1 tsp
water	7 pints	7 pints	4 l
wine yeast			
yeast nutrient			

1. Strip the mulberries from the stalks, crush them well and cover with 5 pints (2.8 l) of boiling water.
2. When cool, add the crushed Camden tablet and pectin enzyme and leave to steep for 24 hours.
3. Bring a further 2 pints (1.1 l) of water to the boil and dissolve the sugar in it.
4. When this syrup has cooled to blood heat, add it to the mulberry pulp together with the yeast and nutrient.
5. Cover well and leave in a warm place to ferment for 3 days, stirring twice daily.
6. Strain the liquid off the pulp and measure, if necessary adding cool boiled water to make up to 1 gallon (4.5 l).
7. Transfer to a fermenting jar, fit bung and air-lock and leave to ferment on, racking when the wine starts to clear.
8. When the fermentation has finished working and the wine has cleared, bottle and store in a cool dark place to mature for at least 9 months, preferably 1 year.

RASPBERRY

Ripe raspberries, preferably gathered during a warm, dry spell of weather, make a delicious rosé wine with a distinctive fruity flavour and bouquet. The fruit tends to be acid so don't overdo the amount used.

	IMP	US	METRIC
ripe raspberries	3 lbs	2½ lbs	1.4 kg
sugar	3 lbs	2½ lbs	1.4 kg
Camden tablets	1½	1½	1½
pectin enzyme	1 tsp	1 tsp	1 tsp
water	7 pints	7 pints	4 l
wine yeast			
yeast nutrient			

1. Wash the raspberries thoroughly to remove any maggots. Crush the fruit and cover with 5 pints (2.8 l) of boiling water.

2. When this has cooled, stir in the crushed Camden tablet and pectin enzyme, and leave to steep for 48 hours, stirring occasionally.

3. Strain the liquid from the raspberry pulp, pressing well to extract as much juice as possible. Measure, and if necessary make up to 6 pints (3.4 l) with cool boiled water.

4. Bring a further 2 pints (1.1 l) of water to the boil and dissolve the sugar in it.

5. When this syrup has cooled, add it to the raspberry liquid together with the yeast and nutrient.

6. Cover well and leave in a warm place to ferment for 4 days, stirring twice daily.

7. Transfer to a fermenting jar, fit bung and air-lock and leave to ferment on, racking when the wine is beginning to clear.
8. When all fermentation has ceased and the wine is cleared completely, bottle and store in a cool dark place to mature for at least 6 months.
9. This recipe can also be used to make Raspberry & Red Currant wine, using 2 lbs raspberries and 2 lbs red currants (1¾ lbs: 1¾ lbs US; 905 g: 905 g).

ROSEHIP

Hips, or heps, are the fruit of the rose and are traditionally gathered after the first frost of November. This is a most beneficial wine to make, as the ripened hips are rich in vitamin C.

	IMP	US	METRIC
ripe rosehips	4 lbs	3¼ lbs	1.8 kg
sugar	3½ lbs	3 lbs	1.6 kg
lemon	1	1	1
Camden tablet	1	1	1
pectin enzyme	1 tsp	1 tsp	1 tsp
water	1 gallon	1 gallon	4.5 l
wine yeast			
yeast nutrient			

1. Put the washed hips into a vessel and crush well with a mallet or similar implement.
2. Cover with 1 gallon (4.5 l) of cold water, stir in the crushed Camden tablet and pectin enzyme and leave to steep for 24 hours.
3. Draw off 2 pints (1.1 l) of the liquid, heat just to boiling point and dissolve the sugar in it.
4. Return this syrup when cooled to the rosehip pulp, together with the yeast, nutrient and juice of the lemon.
5. Cover the vessel and leave in a warm place to ferment for 5 days, stirring twice daily.
6. Strain the liquid off the pulp, pressing well to extract all the juice, and transfer to a fermenting jar. Fit bung and air-lock and leave to ferment on, racking when the wine is starting to clear.
7. When all fermentation has ended and the wine is quite clear, bottle and store in a cool dark place to mature for at least 6 months, preferably a little longer.

ROWANBERRY

The scarlet berries of the rowan, or mountain ash tree, make a pleasant autumn wine. Pick the berries on a warm dry day – and don't delay once they're ripe, or the birds will beat you to it.

	IMP	US	METRIC
ripe rowanberries	4 lbs	3¼ lbs	1.8 kg
sugar	3 lbs	2½ lbs	1.4 kg
raisins	8 ozs	7 ozs	226 g
root ginger	1 oz	7/8 oz	28 g
lemons	2	2	2
Camden tablet	1	1	1
pectin enzyme	1 tsp	1 tsp	1 tsp
water	1 gallon	1 gallon	4.5 l
wine yeast			
yeast nutrient			

1. Put the berries into a vessel, crush well and cover with 6 pints (3.4 l) of boiling water.
2. Allow to cool, stir in the Camden tablet and pectin enzyme, and leave to steep for 48 hours, stirring occasionally.
3. Bring a further 2 pints (1.1 l) of water to the boil and dissolve the sugar in it.
4. Let this syrup cool to blood heat, then add to the pulp together with the yeast and nutrient, the juice of the lemons, the chopped raisins and bruised ginger.
5. Cover the vessel and leave in a warm place to ferment for 4 days, stirring twice daily.
6. Strain the liquid off the pulp and transfer to a fermenting jar. Close off with an air-lock and leave to ferment on, racking when the wine starts to clear.
7. When the fermentation has finished working and the wine has cleared, bottle and store in a cool dark place to mature for at least 9 months.

SLOE

Sloes are the blue-black autumn berries of the black-thorn shrub. They should be gathered in October when they're at their ripest – even slightly over-ripe – otherwise the high acid and tannin content of the immature fruit will spoil the wine. Sloe wine takes a year or two to mature, but the wait is well worth it.

	IMP	US	METRIC
ripe sloes	3 lbs	2½ lbs	1.4 kg
sugar	3 lbs	2½ lbs	1.4 kg
raisins	8 ozs	7 ozs	226 g
Camden tablet	1	1	1
pectin enzyme	1 tsp	1 tsp	1 tsp
water	1 gallon	1 gallon	4.5 l
wine yeast			
yeast nutrient			

1. Wash the sloes, put them into a vessel and pulp them. Cover with 6 pints (3.4 l) of cold water, add the crushed Camden tablet and pectin enzyme, and leave to steep for 24 hours.
2. Bring a further 2 pints (1.1 l) of water to the boil and pour over the sugar, stirring well until dissolved.
3. When this syrup has cooled to blood heat, add it to the sloe pulp together with the yeast and nutrient and chopped raisins.
4. Cover well and leave to ferment in a warm place for 3–4 days, stirring twice daily.
5. Strain the liquid off the pulp, pressing well to extract as much juice as possible. Transfer to a fermenting jar, fit bung and air-lock and leave to ferment on, racking when the wine starts clearing.
6. When all fermentation has ceased and the wine cleared completely, bottle and store in a cool dark place to mature. This wine is drinkable after 1 year, but is much better if left for 2 years, and preferably 3.

TRIUMPH PEACH.
EARLIEST AND MOST PROFITABLE
YELLOW PEACH. HARDY AND RELIABLE
SEE INSIDE
COVER
PAGE

SUNRISE
CHERRY
EXTRA EARLY
PRODUCTIVE

HALE PLUM
HIGHEST
QUALITY
MOST
BEAUTIFUL
OF THE
JAPAN PLUMS

All these fruits
photographed in colors
for
G.H. AND J.H. HALE
SOUTH GLASTONBURY
CONNECTICUT

STRAWBERRY

Make sure the fruit is well ripened, even slightly squashy so long as it isn't damaged, and gather on a warm dry day. Ferment in a darkened glass jar if possible to preserve the attractive rose colour.

	IMP	US	METRIC
ripe strawberries	5 lbs	4½ lbs	2.3 kg
sugar	3 lbs	2½ lbs	1.4 kg
lemon	1	1	1
Camden tablets	2	2	2
pectin enzyme	1 tsp	1 tsp	1 tsp
grape tannin	½ tsp	½ tsp	½ tsp
water	1 gallon	1 gallon	4.5 l
wine yeast			
yeast nutrient			

1. Wash the strawberries, remove the green caps and crush the fruit in a vessel. Pour over sufficient cold water to cover (about 4 pints, or 2.25 l), add the crushed Camden tablets and pectin enzyme, and leave for 48 hours, stirring occasionally.
2. Strain the liquid off the pulp, pressing well to extract all the juice. Measure the liquid and if necessary add cool boiled water to make up to 6 pints (3.4 l).
3. Bring a further 2 pints (1.1 l) of water to the boil and pour over the sugar, stirring until dissolved.
4. Allow this syrup to cool, then add to the strawberry liquid together with the yeast and nutrient, the grape tannin and the lemon juice.
5. Cover the vessel well and leave in a warm place to ferment for 3 days, stirring twice daily.
6. Transfer to a fermenting jar, close off with an air-lock and leave to ferment on, racking when the wine starts to clear.
7. When all fermentation has ended and the wine has cleared, bottle and store in a cool dark place to mature for at least 6 months.

FLOWER
WINES

BROOM (OR GORSE)

Flowers, or blossoms, are amongst the easiest and most rewarding material to use for wine-making. They clear well, mature early, and produce wines of delicate flavour and pleasantly fragrant bouquet. Pick the blossoms when they're in full bloom, on a dry sunny day, and discard stems and other green parts. To measure the amount required, pack the flower heads loosely into a measuring jug.

	IMP	US	METRIC
broom flowers	1 gallon	1 gallon	4.5 l
sugar	2½ lbs	2 lbs	1.2 kg
sultanas	8 ozs	7 ozs	226 g
lemons	3	3	3
Camden tablet	1	1	1
grape tannin	½ tsp	½ tsp	½ tsp
water	1 gallon	1 gallon	4.5 l
wine yeast			
yeast nutrient			

1. Wash the blossom well to remove dust and insects, put into a vessel and cover with 1 gallon (4.5 l) of boiling water.
2. Stir in the crushed Camden tablet and leave to infuse for 24 hours. Draw off 2 pints (1.1 l) of the liquid, heat just to boiling point and pour over the sugar, stirring until dissolved.
3. When this syrup has cooled to blood heat, return it to the bulk of the liquid, together with the yeast and nutrient, the chopped sultanas, grape tannin and the juice of the citrus fruit.
4. Cover well and leave in a warm place to ferment for 5 days, stirring twice daily.
5. Strain the liquid carefully and transfer to a fermenting jar. Fit an airlock and leave to ferment on, racking when the wine starts to clear.
6. When all fermentation has ceased and the wine has cleared completely, bottle and store in a cool dark place to mature for at least 4 months.

CARNATION

All flower wines are made by the same method; and being naturally thin in body, they need the addition of dried fruit, citric acid and tannin. Pick the blossoms when they're in full bloom, on a dry sunny day, and discard stems and other green parts. To measure the amount required, pack the flower heads loosely into a measuring jug.

	IMP	US	METRIC
carnation petals	3 pints	3 pints	1.7 l
sugar	2½ lbs	2 lbs	1.2 kg
sultanas	8 ozs	7 ozs	226 g
lemons	2	2	2
Camden tablet	1	1	1
grape tannin	½ tsp	½ tsp	½ tsp
water	1 gallon	1 gallon	4.5 l
wine yeast			
yeast nutrient			

1. Wash the blossom well to remove dust and insects, put into a vessel and cover with 1 gallon (4.5 l) of boiling water.
2. Stir in the crushed Camden tablet and leave to infuse for 24 hours. Draw off 2 pints (1.1 l) of the liquid, heat just to boiling point and pour over the sugar, stirring until dissolved.
3. When this syrup has cooled to blood heat, return it to the bulk of the liquid, together with the yeast and nutrient, the chopped sultanas, grape tannin and the juice of the citrus fruit.
4. Cover well and leave in a warm place to ferment for 5 days, stirring twice daily.
5. Strain the liquid carefully and transfer to a fermenting jar. Fit an air-lock and leave to ferment on, racking when the wine starts to clear.
6. When all fermentation has ceased and the wine has cleared completely, bottle and store in a cool dark place to mature for at least 4 months.

CLOVER

All flower wines are made by the same method; and being naturally thin in body, they need the addition of dried fruit, citric acid and tannin. Pick the blossoms when they're in full bloom, on a dry sunny day, and discard stems and other green parts. To measure the amount required, pack the flower heads loosely into a measuring jug.

	IMP	US	METRIC
purple clover petals	6 pints	6 pints	3.4 l
sugar	2½ lbs	2 lbs	1.2 kg
sultanas	8 ozs	7 ozs	226 g
lemons	2	2	2
oranges	2	2	2
Camden tablet	1	1	1
grape tannin	½ tsp	½ tsp	½ tsp
water	1 gallon	1 gallon	4.5 l
wine yeast			
yeast nutrient			

1. Wash the blossom well to remove dust and insects, put into a vessel and cover with 1 gallon (4.5 l) of boiling water.
2. Stir in the crushed Camden tablet and leave to infuse for 24 hours. Draw off 2 pints (1.1 l) of the liquid, heat just to boiling point and pour over the sugar, stirring until dissolved.
3. When this syrup has cooled to blood heat, return it to the bulk of the liquid, together with the yeast and nutrient, the chopped sultanas, grape tannin and the juice of the citrus fruit.
4. Cover well and leave in a warm place to ferment for 5 days, stirring twice daily.
5. Strain the liquid carefully and transfer to a fermenting jar. Fit an airlock and leave to ferment on, racking when the wine starts to clear.
6. When all fermentation has ceased and the wine has cleared completely, bottle and store in a cool dark place to mature for at least 4 months.

COLTSFOOT

All flower wines are made by the same method; and being naturally thin in body, they need the addition of dried fruit, citric acid and tannin. Pick the blossoms when they're in full bloom, on a dry sunny day, and discard stems and other green parts. To measure the amount required, pack the flower heads loosely into a measuring jug.

	IMP	US	METRIC
coltsfoot flowers	1 gallon	1 gallon	4.5 l
sugar	2½ lbs	2 lbs	1.2 kg
sultanas	8 ozs	7 ozs	226 g
lemons	2	2	2
oranges	2	2	2
Camden tablet	1	1	1
grape tannin	½ tsp	½ tsp	½ tsp
water	1 gallon	1 gallon	4.5 l
wine yeast			
yeast nutrient			

1. Wash the blossom well to remove dust and insects, put into a vessel and cover with 1 gallon (4.5 l) of boiling water.
2. Stir in the crushed Camden tablet and leave to infuse for 24 hours. Draw off 2 pints (1.1 l) of the liquid, heat just to boiling point and pour over the sugar, stirring until dissolved.
3. When this syrup has cooled to blood heat, return it to the bulk of the liquid, together with the yeast and nutrient, the chopped sultanas, grape tannin and the juice of the citrus fruit.
4. Cover well and leave in a warm place to ferment for 5 days, stirring twice daily.
5. Strain the liquid carefully and transfer to a fermenting jar. Fit an air-lock and leave to ferment on, racking when the wine starts to clear.
6. When all fermentation has ceased and the wine has cleared completely, bottle and store in a cool dark place to mature for at least 4 months.

COWSLIP

All flower wines are made by the same method; and being naturally thin in body, they need the addition of dried fruit, citric acid and tannin. Pick the blossoms when they're in full bloom, on a dry sunny day, and discard stems and other green parts. To measure the amount required, pack the flower heads loosely into a measuring jug.

	IMP	US	METRIC
cowslip flowers	6 pints	6 pints	3.4 l
sugar	2½ lbs	2 lbs	1.2 kg
sultanas	8 ozs	7 ozs	226 g
lemons	2	2	2
Camden tablet	1	1	1
grape tannin	½ tsp	½ tsp	½ tsp
water	1 gallon	1 gallon	4.5 l
wine yeast			
yeast nutrient			

1. Wash the blossom well to remove dust and insects, put into a vessel and cover with 1 gallon (4.5 l) of boiling water.
2. Stir in the crushed Camden tablet and leave to infuse for 24 hours. Draw off 2 pints (1.1 l) of the liquid, heat just to boiling point and pour over the sugar, stirring until dissolved.
3. When this syrup has cooled to blood heat, return it to the bulk of the liquid, together with the yeast and nutrient, the chopped sultanas, grape tannin and the juice of the citrus fruit.
4. Cover well and leave in a warm place to ferment for 5 days, stirring twice daily.
5. Strain the liquid carefully and transfer to a fermenting jar. Fit an airlock and leave to ferment on, racking when the wine starts to clear.
6. When all fermentation has ceased and the wine has cleared completely, bottle and store in a cool dark place to mature for at least 4 months.

DANDELION

All flower wines are made by the same method; and being naturally thin in body, they need the addition of dried fruit, citric acid and tannin. Pick the blossoms when they're in full bloom, on a dry sunny day, and discard stems and other green parts. To measure the amount required, pack the flower heads loosely into a measuring jug.

	IMP	US	METRIC
dandelion petals	4 pints	4 pints	2.25 l
sugar	2½ lbs	2 lbs	1.2 kg
sultanas	8 ozs	7 ozs	226 g
lemons	2	2	2
orange	1	1	1
Camden tablet	1	1	1
grape tannin	½ tsp	½ tsp	½ tsp
water	1 gallon	1 gallon	4.5 l
wine yeast			
yeast nutrient			

1. Wash the blossom well to remove dust and insects, put into a vessel and cover with 1 gallon (4.5 l) of boiling water.
2. Stir in the crushed Camden tablet and leave to infuse for 24 hours. Draw off 2 pints (1.1 l) of the liquid, heat just to boiling point and pour over the sugar, stirring until dissolved.
3. When this syrup has cooled to blood heat, return it to the bulk of the liquid, together with the yeast and nutrient, the chopped sultanas, grape tannin and the juice of the citrus fruit.
4. Cover well and leave in a warm place to ferment for 5 days, stirring twice daily.
5. Strain the liquid carefully and transfer to a fermenting jar. Fit an air-lock and leave to ferment on, racking when the wine starts to clear.
6. When all fermentation has ceased and the wine has cleared completely, bottle and store in a cool dark place to mature for at least 4 months.

ELDERFLOWER

All flower wines are made by the same method; and being naturally thin in body, they need the addition of dried fruit, citric acid and tannin. Pick the blossoms when they're in full bloom, on a dry sunny day, and discard stems and other green parts. To measure the amount required, pack the flower heads loosely into a measuring jug.

	IMP	US	METRIC
elderflowers	1 pint	1 pint	568 ml
sugar	2½lbs	2 lbs	1.2 kg
sultanas	8 ozs	7 ozs	226 g
lemons	2	2	2
Camden tablet	1	1	1
grape tannin	½ tsp	½ tsp	½ tsp
water	1 gallon	1 gallon	4.5 l
wine yeast			
yeast nutrient			

1. Wash the blossom well to remove dust and insects, put into a vessel and cover with 1 gallon (4.5 l) of boiling water.
2. Stir in the crushed Camden tablet and leave to infuse for 24 hours. Draw off 2 pints (1.1 l) of the liquid, heat just to boiling point and pour over the sugar, stirring until dissolved.
3. When this syrup has cooled to blood heat, return it to the bulk of the liquid, together with the yeast and nutrient, the chopped sultanas, grape tannin and the juice of the citrus fruit.
4. Cover well and leave in a warm place to ferment for 5 days, stirring twice daily.
5. Strain the liquid carefully and transfer to a fermenting jar. Fit an airlock and leave to ferment on, racking when the wine starts to clear.
6. When all fermentation has ceased and the wine has cleared completely, bottle and store in a cool dark place to mature for at least 4 months.

GOLDEN ROD

All flower wines are made by the same method; and being naturally thin in body, they need the addition of dried fruit, citric acid and tannin. Pick the blossoms when they're in full bloom, on a dry sunny day, and discard stems and other green parts. To measure the amount required, pack the flower heads loosely into a measuring jug.

	IMP	US	METRIC
golden rod flowers	2 pints	2 pints	1.1 l
sugar	2½ lbs	2 lbs	1.2 kg
sultanas	8 ozs	7 ozs	226 g
lemons	2	2	2
Camden tablet	1	1	1
grape tannin	½ tsp	½ tsp	½ tsp
water	1 gallon	1 gallon	4.5 l
wine yeast			
yeast nutrient			

1. Wash the blossom well to remove dust and insects, put into a vessel and cover with 1 gallon (4.5 l) of boiling water.
2. Stir in the crushed Camden tablet and leave to infuse for 24 hours. Draw off 2 pints (1.1 l) of the liquid, heat just to boiling point and pour over the sugar, stirring until dissolved.
3. When this syrup has cooled to blood heat, return it to the bulk of the liquid, together with the yeast and nutrient, the chopped sultanas, grape tannin and the juice of the citrus fruit.
4. Cover well and leave in a warm place to ferment for 5 days, stirring twice daily.
5. Strain the liquid carefully and transfer to a fermenting jar. Fit an air-lock and leave to ferment on, racking when the wine starts to clear.
6. When all fermentation has ceased and the wine has cleared completely, bottle and store in a cool dark place to mature for at least 4 months.

HAWTHORN BLOSSOM (OR MAYFLOWER)

All flower wines are made by the same method; and being naturally thin in body, they need the addition of dried fruit, citric acid and tannin. Pick the blossoms when they're in full bloom, on a dry sunny day, and discard stems and other green parts. To measure the amount required, pack the flower heads loosely into a measuring jug.

	IMP	US	METRIC
hawthorn blossom	4 pints	4 pints	2.25 l
sugar	2½ lbs	2 lbs	1.2 kg
sultanas	8 ozs	7 ozs	226 g
lemons	2	2	2
Camden tablet	1	1	1
grape tannin	½ tsp	½ tsp	½ tsp
water	1 gallon	1 gallon	4.5 l
wine yeast			
yeast nutrient			

1. Wash the blossom well to remove dust and insects, put into a vessel and cover with 1 gallon (4.5 l) of boiling water.
2. Stir in the crushed Camden tablet and leave to infuse for 24 hours. Draw off 2 pints (1.1 l) of the liquid, heat just to boiling point and pour over the sugar, stirring until dissolved.
3. When this syrup has cooled to blood heat, return it to the bulk of the liquid, together with the yeast and nutrient, the chopped sultanas, grape tannin and the juice of the citrus fruit.
4. Cover well and leave in a warm place to ferment for 5 days, stirring twice daily.
5. Strain the liquid carefully and transfer to a fermenting jar. Fit an airlock and leave to ferment on, racking when the wine starts to clear.
6. When all fermentation has ceased and the wine has cleared completely, bottle and store in a cool dark place to mature for at least 4 months.

HONEYSUCKLE

All flower wines are made by the same method; and being naturally thin in body, they need the addition of dried fruit, citric acid and tannin. Pick the blossoms when they're in full bloom, on a dry sunny day, and discard stems and other green parts. To measure the amount required, pack the flower heads loosely into a measuring jug.

	IMP	US	METRIC
honeysuckle flowers	3 pints	3 pints	1.7 l
sugar	2½ lbs	2 lbs	1.2 kg
sultanas	8 ozs	7 ozs	226 g
lemons	2	2	2
Camden tablet	1	1	1
grape tannin	½ tsp	½ tsp	½ tsp
water	1 gallon	1 gallon	4.5 l
wine yeast			
yeast nutrient			

1. Wash the blossom well to remove dust and insects, put into a vessel and cover with 1 gallon (4.5 l) of boiling water.
2. Stir in the crushed Camden tablet and leave to infuse for 24 hours. Draw off 2 pints (1.1 l) of the liquid, heat just to boiling point and pour over the sugar, stirring until dissolved.
3. When this syrup has cooled to blood heat, return it to the bulk of the liquid, together with the yeast and nutrient, the chopped sultanas, grape tannin and the juice of the citrus fruit.
4. Cover well and leave in a warm place to ferment for 5 days, stirring twice daily.
5. Strain the liquid carefully and transfer to a fermenting jar. Fit an airlock and leave to ferment on, racking when the wine starts to clear.
6. When all fermentation has ceased and the wine has cleared completely, bottle and store in a cool dark place to mature for at least 4 months.

LIME BLOSSOM (OR LINDEN BLOSSOM)

All flower wines are made by the same method; and being naturally thin in body, they need the addition of dried fruit, citric acid and tannin. Pick the blossoms when they're in full bloom, on a dry sunny day, and discard stems and other green parts. To measure the amount required, pack the flower heads loosely into a measuring jug.

	IMP	US	METRIC
lime, or linden blossom	3 pints	3 pints	1.7 l
sugar	2½ lbs	2 lbs	1.2 kg
sultanas	8 ozs	7 ozs	226 g
lemons	2	2	2
Camden tablet	1	1	1
grape tannin	½ tsp	½ tsp	½ tsp
water	1 gallon	1 gallon	4.5 l
wine yeast			
yeast nutrient			

1. Wash the blossom well to remove dust and insects, put into a vessel and cover with 1 gallon (4.5 l) of boiling water.
2. Stir in the crushed Camden tablet and leave to infuse for 24 hours. Draw off 2 pints (1.1 l) of the liquid, heat just to boiling point and pour over the sugar, stirring until dissolved.
3. When this syrup has cooled to blood heat, return it to the bulk of the liquid, together with the yeast and nutrient, the chopped sultanas, grape tannin and the juice of the citrus fruit.
4. Cover well and leave in a warm place to ferment for 5 days, stirring twice daily.
5. Strain the liquid carefully and transfer to a fermenting jar. Fit an air-lock and leave to ferment on, racking when the wine starts to clear.
6. When all fermentation has ceased and the wine has cleared completely, bottle and store in a cool dark place to mature for at least 4 months.

MARIGOLD

All flower wines are made by the same method; and being naturally thin in body, they need the addition of dried fruit, citric acid and tannin. Pick the blossoms when they're in full bloom, on a dry sunny day, and discard stems and other green parts. To measure the amount required, pack the flower heads loosely into a measuring jug.

	IMP	US	METRIC
marigold petals	3 pints	3 pints	1.7 l
sugar	2½ lbs	2 lbs	1.2 kg
sultanas	8 ozs	7 ozs	226 g
lemon	1	1	1
oranges	2	2	2
Camden tablet	1	1	1
grape tannin	½ tsp	½ tsp	½ tsp
water	1 gallon	1 gallon	4.5 l
wine yeast			
yeast nutrient			

1. Wash the blossom well to remove dust and insects, put into a vessel and cover with 1 gallon (4.5 l) of boiling water.
2. Stir in the crushed Camden tablet and leave to infuse for 24 hours. Draw off 2 pints (1.1 l) of the liquid, heat just to boiling point and pour over the sugar, stirring until dissolved.
3. When this syrup has cooled to blood heat, return it to the bulk of the liquid, together with the yeast and nutrient, the chopped sultanas, grape tannin and the juice of the citrus fruit.
4. Cover well and leave in a warm place to ferment for 5 days, stirring twice daily.
5. Strain the liquid carefully and transfer to a fermenting jar. Fit an airlock and leave to ferment on, racking when the wine starts to clear.
6. When all fermentation has ceased and the wine has cleared completely, bottle and store in a cool dark place to mature for at least 4 months.

PRIMROSE

All flower wines are made by the same method; and being naturally thin in body, they need the addition of dried fruit, citric acid and tannin. Pick the blossoms when they're in full bloom, on a dry sunny day, and discard stems and other green parts. To measure the amount required, pack the flower heads loosely into a measuring jug.

	IMP	US	METRIC
primrose flowers	6 pints	6 pints	3.4 l
sugar	2½ lbs	2 lbs	1.2 kg
sultanas	8 ozs	7 ozs	226 g
lemon	1	1	1
oranges	2	2	2
Camden tablet	1	1	1
grape tannin	½ tsp	½ tsp	½ tsp
water	1 gallon	1 gallon	4.5 l
wine yeast			
yeast nutrient			

1. Wash the blossom well to remove dust and insects, put into a vessel and cover with 1 gallon (4.5 l) of boiling water.
2. Stir in the crushed Camden tablet and leave to infuse for 24 hours. Draw off 2 pints (1.1 l) of the liquid, heat just to boiling point and pour over the sugar, stirring until dissolved.
3. When this syrup has cooled to blood heat, return it to the bulk of the liquid, together with the yeast and nutrient, the chopped sultanas, grape tannin and the juice of the citrus fruit.
4. Cover well and leave in a warm place to ferment for 5 days, stirring twice daily.
5. Strain the liquid carefully and transfer to a fermenting jar. Fit an airlock and leave to ferment on, racking when the wine starts to clear.
6. When all fermentation has ceased and the wine has cleared completely, bottle and store in a cool dark place to mature for at least 4 months.

ROSE PETAL

All flower wines are made by the same method; and being naturally thin in body, they need the addition of dried fruit, citric acid and tannin. Pick the blossoms when they're in full bloom, on a dry sunny day, and discard stems and other green parts. To measure the amount required, pack the flower heads loosely into a measuring jug.

	IMP	US	METRIC
rose petals	4 pints	4 pints	2.25 l
sugar	2½lbs	2 lbs	1.2 kg
sultanas	8 ozs	7 ozs	226 g
lemons	2	2	2
Camden tablet	1	1	1
grape tannin	½ tsp	½ tsp	½ tsp
water	1 gallon	1 gallon	4.5 l
wine yeast			
yeast nutrient			

1. Wash the blossom well to remove dust and insects, put into a vessel and cover with 1 gallon (4.5 l) of boiling water.
2. Stir in the crushed Camden tablet and leave to infuse for 24 hours. Draw off 2 pints (1.1 l) of the liquid, heat just to boiling point and pour over the sugar, stirring until dissolved.
3. When this syrup has cooled to blood heat, return it to the bulk of the liquid, together with the yeast and nutrient, the chopped sultanas, grape tannin and the juice of the citrus fruit.
4. Cover well and leave in a warm place to ferment for 5 days, stirring twice daily.
5. Strain the liquid carefully and transfer to a fermenting jar. Fit an airlock and leave to ferment on, racking when the wine starts to clear.
6. When all fermentation has ceased and the wine has cleared completely, bottle and store in a cool dark place to mature for at least 4 months.

HOP

Hops are usually associated with beer, having been used for centuries as a flavouring, but their cone-shaped green heads – the hop flowers – can also be used to make an attractive medium sweet white wine.

	IMP	US	METRIC
fresh hops	2 pints	2 pints	1.1 l
or dried hops	3 ozs	2¾ ozs	85 g
sugar	3 lbs	2½ lbs	1.4 kg
raisins	8 ozs	7 ozs	226 g
root ginger	1 oz	7/8 oz	28 g
oranges	2	2	2
water	1 gallon	1 gallon	4.5 l
wine yeast			
yeast nutrient			

1. Add the hops and bruised ginger to 1 gallon (4.5 l) of water in a boiling vessel. Bring to the boil, cover with a lid and simmer for 1 hour. Strain the liquid on to the sugar and stir well until dissolved.
2. Leave until just comfortably warm before adding the yeast and nutrient, the chopped raisins and the juice of the oranges.
3. Cover and leave in a warm place to ferment for 3 days, stirring twice daily. Strain the liquid into a fermenting jar, fit bung and air-lock and leave to ferment on, racking when the wine starts to clear.
4. When all fermentation has finished and the wine cleared, bottle and store in a cool dark place to mature for at least 6 months.

FRUIT
WINES

APPLE

Use sound, juicy dessert apples – and if you like a wine with a sharp flavour, mix in a few cooking apples. Ideally, a press should be used to extract the juice, but failing this, put the fruit through a coarse mincer.

	IMP	US	METRIC
apples	6 lbs	5¼ lbs	2.7 kg
sugar	3 lbs	2½ lbs	1.4 kg
raisins	8 ozs	7 ozs	226 g
lemons	2	2	2
Camden tablets	2	2	2
water			
wine yeast			
yeast nutrient			

1. Wash the apples without peeling them, cut them up roughly and discard the cores.
2. Pour over sufficient water to cover the pieces, add the crushed Camden tablets and leave to steep for 48 hours, stirring occasionally.
3. Remove the fruit from the liquid and press or mince to extract the juice, taking care that none is lost in the process.
4. Return the juice to the liquid, measure and if necessary make up to 1 gallon (4.5 l) with water.
5. Bring the liquid just to the boil and stir in the sugar until dissolved. Leave until just comfortably warm, then add the yeast and nutrient, the juice of the lemons and the chopped raisins.
6. Cover well and leave to ferment in a warm place for 3–4 days, stirring twice daily.

7. Strain into a fermenting jar, close off with an air-lock and leave to ferment on, racking once the wine starts to clear.
8. When the fermentation has finished working and the wine is clear, bottle and store in a cool dark place to mature. Ready for drinking after 6 months, but improves if kept for a year.

This recipe can be used to make the following variations, adding the extra fruit at stage 1 and reducing the apples to 4 lbs (3¼ lbs US; 1.8 kg):

Blackberry & Apple (blackberries 2 lbs; 1¾ lbs US; 905 g); Cranberry & Apple (cranberries 2 lbs; 1¾ lbs US; 905 g); Elderberry & Apple (elderberries 1½ lbs; 1½ lbs US; 679 g); Plum & Apple (stoned plums 2 lbs; 1¾ lbs US; 905 g); Quince & Apple (quinces 2 lbs; 1¾ lbs US; 905 g); Sloe & Apple (sloes 1 lb; 14 ozs US; 453 g).

APRICOT

Apricots make a pleasant dry white wine, considered to be one of the
best of the home-made wines. Like all stone fruit, they contain a lot of
pectin and a pectin-reducing enzyme must be used or the wine will
be difficult to clear. This recipe can also be used to make wine from
nectarines.

	IMP	US	METRIC
fresh apricots	4 lbs	3¼ lbs	1.8 kg
sugar	2½ lbs	2 lbs	1.2 kg
Camden tablet	1	1	1
pectin enzyme	2 tsps	2 tsps	2 tsps
water	1 gallon	1 gallon	4.5 l
wine yeast			
yeast nutrient			

1. Halve the apricots, removing the stones but not the skins. Crush
   the fruit well until pulpy. Cover with 6 pints (3.4 l) of cold water,
   add the crushed Camden tablet and pectin enzyme, and leave to
   steep for 24 hours.
2. Bring a further 2 pints (1.1 l) of water to the boil and dissolve the
   sugar thoroughly in it.
3. Allow this syrup to cool to blood heat, then add to the apricot pulp
   together with the yeast and nutrient.
4. Cover and keep in a warm place to ferment for 7 days, stirring twice
   daily. Strain the liquid off the pulp and transfer to a fermenting jar.
   Close off with an air-lock and leave to ferment on, racking when the
   wine begins to clear.
5. When all fermentation has ceased and the wine has cleared
   completely, bottle and store in a cool dark place to mature for at
   least 6 months.

BANANA

This makes a strong, sweet white wine. Bananas contain a lot of starch, so use a cereal wine yeast to reduce the starch haze or the wine will be cloudy. Choose fruit that is really ripe: spotted or even black bananas are best.

	IMP	US	METRIC
ripe bananas	4 lbs	3¼ lbs	1.8 kg
banana skins	2	2	2
sugar	3 lbs	2½ lbs	1.4 kg
raisins	8 ozs	7 ozs	226 g
lemon	1	1	1
orange	1	1	1
grape tannin	½ tsp	½ tsp	½ tsp
water	1 gallon	1 gallon	4.5 l
cereal wine yeast			
yeast nutrient			

1. Peel the bananas and slice into 1 gallon (4.5 l) of water with a little thinly peeled citrus rind (avoiding the white pith) and the banana skins.
2. Bring to the boil, cover and simmer for 30 minutes.
3. Strain the liquid on to the sugar, pressing the banana pulp well to extract as much moisture as possible. Stir well to dissolve the sugar.
4. Leave until comfortably warm, then add the yeast and nutrient, the chopped raisins, grape tannin and juice of the citrus fruits.
5. Cover and leave to ferment in a warm place for 5 days, stirring twice daily. Strain carefully into a fermenting jar, fit bung and air-lock and leave to ferment on, racking regularly as the sediment builds up.
6. When the fermentation has ended and the wine has cleared, bottle and store in a cool dark place to mature. This wine may be drunk after 6 months but improves the longer it is kept.

BULLACE

Bullaces are an old-fashioned damsons. They are very bitter and are best made as a sweet wine, requiring a longer maturing period than most home-made wines.

	IMP	US	METRIC
ripe bullaces	4 lbs	3¼ lbs	1.8 kg
sugar	3½ lbs	3 lbs	1.6 kg
Camden tablet	1	1	1
pectin enzyme	2 tsps	2 tsps	2 tsps
water	1 gallon	1 gallon	4.5 l
wine yeast			
yeast nutrient			

1. Put the washed fruit into a vessel and crush well, taking care not to break the stones. Cover with 6 pints (3.4 l) of cold water, add the crushed Camden tablet and pectin enzyme, and leave to steep for 24 hours.
2. Bring a further 2 pints (1.1 l) of water to the boil and dissolve the sugar in it.
3. When this syrup has cooled to blood heat, stir it into the bullace pulp, then add the yeast and nutrient.
4. Cover and leave to ferment in a warm place for 3 days, stirring twice daily. Strain the liquid off the bullaces, pressing the pulp well, and transfer to a fermenting jar. Fit an air-lock and leave to ferment on, racking when the wine begins to clear.
5. When all fermentation has ended and the wine cleared, bottle and store in a cool dark place to mature for at least a year, preferably 2 years.

CHERRY

The sour Morello cherry is best for this wine and has enough natural acid not to need any addition. If you can't get Morellos, use black dessert cherries – they're second-best, but still produce an attractive red wine.

	IMP	US	METRIC
ripe cherries	6 lbs	5¼ lbs	2.7 kg
sugar	3 lbs	2½ lbs	1.4 kg
Camden tablet	1	1	1
pectin enzyme	2 tsps	2 tsps	2 tsps
water	1 gallon	1 gallon	4.5 l
wine yeast			
yeast nutrient			

1. Put the washed cherries into a vessel and crush them, taking care not to break the stones. Cover with 6 pints (3.4 l) of boiling water and when this has cooled, stir in the crushed Camden tablet and pectin enzyme.
2. Cover and leave to steep for 48 hours, stirring occasionally.
3. Strain the liquid off the pulp, pressing well to extract all the juice. Bring a further 2 pints (1.1 l) of water to the boil and dissolve the sugar in it.
4. When this syrup has cooled to blood heat, add it to the cherry pulp, followed by the yeast and nutrient (and for black dessert cherries only, the juice of two lemons).
5. Cover well and stand in a warm place to ferment for 4 days, stirring twice daily.
6. Strain into a fermenting jar, close off with an air-lock and leave to ferment on, racking when the wine starts to clear.
7. When all fermentation has ceased and the wine completely cleared, bottle and store in a cool dark place to mature for at least 6 months.
8. An interesting variation is cherry and apricot, using 4 lbs cherries to 2 lbs apricots (3¼ lbs: 1¾ lbs US; 1.8 kg: 905 g).

CITRUS FRUIT

If you grow your own citrus fruits, pick them during the winter months – they can be left on the trees without harm until you need them. Only the juice of the fruits must be used for this wine. The oils in the rind would leave an unpleasantly harsh taste, so avoid including any of the outer part.

	IMP	US	METRIC
grapefruits	3	3	3
lemons	3	3	3
oranges	3	3	3
sugar	3 lbs	2½ lbs	1.4 kg
sultanas	1 lb	14 ozs	453 g
Camden tablet	1	1	1
pectin enzyme	1 tsp	1 tsp	1 tsp
water			
wine yeast			
yeast nutrient			

1. Cut the fruit in half and press out the juice, leaving in any fruit pulp but discarding the pips.
2. Measure the juice and make up to 6 pints (3.4 l) with cold water. Add the crushed Camden tablet and pectin enzyme and leave to stand overnight. Heat a further 2 pints (1.1 l) of water to boiling point and dissolve the sugar in it. When this syrup has cooled to blood heat, add it to the citrus liquid together with the yeast, nutrient and minced sultanas.
3. Cover well and leave to ferment in a warm place for 5–6 days, stirring twice daily.
4. Strain into a fermenting jar, close off with an air-lock and leave to ferment on, racking when the wine begins to clear.
5. When all fermentation has ended and the wine cleared, bottle and store in a cool dark place to mature for at least 6 months.

CLEMENTINE

This recipe will do equally well for any variety of small, sweet, loose-skinned oranges – satsumas, mandarins, tangerines, etc.

	IMP	US	METRIC
tangerines	15–20	15–20	15–20
sugar	3 lbs	2½ lbs	1.4 kg
lemon	1	1	1
Camden tablet	1	1	1
pectin enzyme	1 tsp	1 tsp	1 tsp
grape tannin	½ tsp	½ tsp	½ tsp
water	7 pints	7 pints	4 l
wine yeast			
yeast nutrient			

1. Peel the clementines and carefully remove all white pith and any pips. Put the fruit into a vessel and crush thoroughly.
2. Cover the pulp with 5 pints (2.8 l) of cold water, add the crushed Camden tablet and pectin enzyme and leave to steep for 24 hours.
3. Strain the liquid off the pulp, pressing well to extract all the juice.
4. Measure and if necessary add cool boiled water to make up to 6 pints (3.4 l).
5. Heat a further 2 pints (1.1 l) of water to boiling point and dissolve the sugar in it. When this syrup has cooled, add it to the tangerine liquid together with the yeast and nutrient, the tannin and juice of the lemon. Cover and leave to ferment in a warm place for 4 days, stirring twice daily. Transfer to a fermenting jar, fit bung and air-lock and leave to ferment on, racking when the wine starts to clear.
6. When the fermentation has ended and the wine completely cleared, bottle and store in a cool dark place to mature for at least 6 months.

CRAB APPLE

Crabs are the small, bitter fruit of the wild apple tree and look rather like yellow or red rosehips. The name probably comes from the Swedish skrabba: a wild apple. Because of their astringency, they make a better dry wine than sweet.

	IMP	US	METRIC
crab apples	3 lbs	2½ lbs	1.4 kg
sugar	2¼ lbs	1¾ lbs	1.1 kg
sultanas	1 lb	14 ozs	453 g
oranges	2	2	2
Camden tablet	1	1	1
pectin enzyme	1 tsp	1 tsp	1 tsp
water			
wine yeast			
yeast nutrient			

1. Chop the apples roughly, without peeling or coring, and put into a vessel. Pour over sufficient cold water to cover, stir in the crushed Camden tablet and pectin enzyme, and leave to steep for 48 hours, stirring occasionally.
2. Press the crab apples well to extract as much juice as possible, measure the liquid and make up to 1 gallon (4.5 l) with water.
3. Bring just to boiling point, then pour over the sugar and stir until dissolved.
4. Leave until just comfortably warm, then add the yeast and nutrient, the chopped sultanas and the orange juice. ·
5. Cover well and keep in a warm place to ferment for 6 days, stirring twice daily.
6. Strain into a fermenting jar, fit an air-lock and leave to ferment on, racking when the wine starts to clear.
7. When all fermentation has ceased and the wine has cleared, bottle and store in a cool dark place to mature for at least one year.

DAMSON

Damsons produce a dark red wine with a rich plummy flavour, best fermented in a dark or opaque glass jar to preserve the colour. Like all stone fruits, they need a pectin reducing enzyme to help the wine to clear.

	IMP	US	METRIC
ripe damsons	4 lbs	3¼ lbs	1.8 kg
sugar	3 lbs	2½ lbs	1.4 kg
Camden tablet	1	1	1
pectin enzyme	2 tsps	2 tsps	2 tsps
water	1 gallon	1 gallon	4.5 l
wine yeast			
yeast nutrient			

1. Put the washed fruit into a vessel and bruise it well, taking care not to break any stones.
2. Cover with 6 pints (3.4 l) of boiling water, leave to cool, then stir in the crushed Camden tablet and pectin enzyme. Leave to steep for 24 hours, and at the end of this period pick out as many damson stones as possible. Bring a further 2 pints (1.1 l) of water to the boil and stir in the sugar. When this syrup has cooled, add it to the damson pulp together with the yeast and nutrient.
3. Cover well and leave in a warm place to ferment for 4 days, stirring twice daily.
4. Strain the liquid off the pulp and transfer to a fermenting jar. Close off with bung and air-lock and leave to ferment on, racking when the wine starts to clear.
5. When all fermentation has ended and the wine has cleared completely, bottle and store in a cool dark place to mature. Plum wine needs at least 1 year before it is drinkable, and mellows the longer it is kept.

FIG

Figs, belonging to the mulberry family, have a naturally high sugar content and are best made into a sweet dessert wine.

	IMP	US	METRIC
fresh figs	5 lbs	4½ lbs	2.3 kg
sugar	2 lbs	1¾ lbs	905 g
sultanas	8 ozs	7 ozs	226 g
lemons	2	2	2
orange	1	1	1
Camden tablet	1	1	1
pectin enzyme	2 tsps	2 tsps	2 tsps
grape tannin	½ tsp	½ tsp	½ tsp
water	1 gallon	1 gallon	4.5 l
wine yeast			
yeast nutrient			

1. Put the washed figs into a vessel and mash well. Cover with 6 pints (3.4 l) of boiling water, add the crushed Camden tablet and pectin enzyme when cool, and leave to steep for 48 hours, stirring occasionally.
2. Strain the liquid from the pulp, pressing well to extract all the juice.
3. Bring a further 2 pints (1.1 l) of water to the boil and dissolve the sugar in it.
4. When this syrup has cooled to blood heat, add it to the fig liquid together with the yeast and nutrient, the grape tannin, chopped sultanas and juice of the citrus fruits.
5. Cover well and leave to ferment in a warm place for 4 days, stirring twice daily.
6. Strain the liquid into a fermenting jar, fit bung and air-lock and leave to ferment on, racking when the wine begins to clear.
7. When all fermentation has ceased and the wine has cleared completely, bottle and store in a cool dark place to mature for at least 6 months.

GRAPE WHITE WINE

Small wine grapes are the best kind to use – the larger dessert grapes don't give such a satisfactory result. Pick the fruit from the bunch when they're at their ripest, and discard any that are mouldy or unsound. Many nurseries now sell grapevines of wine varieties suitable for the British climate.

	IMP	US	METRIC
green or amber grapes	20 lbs	17½ lbs	9 kg
sugar	8 ozs	7 ozs	226 g
Camden tablet	1	1	1
wine yeast			
yeast nutrient			

1. Put the washed fruit into a large vessel and crush thoroughly to extract as much juice as possible. Avoid damaging the pips.
2. Strain the juice from the pulp, measure it and if necessary make up to 1 gallon (4.5 l) with cold water.
3. Stir in the crushed Camden tablet, cover and leave for 24 hours.
4. Draw off 1 pint (568 ml) of juice, heat it just to boiling point and dissolve the sugar in it.
5. Return this syrup to the bulk of the liquid, then add the yeast and nutrient.
6. Cover closely and leave to ferment in a warm place for 5 days, stirring twice daily.
7. Transfer to a fermenting jar, close off with an air-lock and leave to ferment on, racking when the wine starts to clear.
8. When fermentation has ended and the wine is completely clear, bottle and store in a cool dark place to mature for at least 2 years.

GRAPE RED WINE

	IMP	US	METRIC
black grapes	20 lbs	17½ lbs	9 kg
sugar	8 ozs	7 ozs	226 g
Camden tablets	2	2	2
pectin enzyme	1 tsp	1 tsp	1 tsp
wine yeast			
yeast nutrient			

1. Put the washed fruit into a large container and crush thoroughly to extract as much juice as possible. Avoid damaging the pips.
2. Dissolve the Camden tablets in an eggcupful of warm water and stir into the pulp, together with the pectin enzyme. Cover and leave for 24 hours. Draw off 1 pint (568 ml) of juice, heat it just to boiling point and dissolve the sugar in it.
3. Return this syrup to the bulk, then add the yeast and nutrient.
4. Cover well and leave to ferment in a warm place for 6 days, stirring twice daily.
5. Strain the liquid off the pulp and transfer to a fermenting jar. Fit an air-lock and leave to ferment on, racking when the wine starts to clear. When all fermentation has ceased and the wine is clear, bottle and store in a cool dark place to mature for at least 2 years, preferably 3 years.
6. This last recipe can also be used to make the following variations, adding the extra fruit at stage 1 and reducing the quantity of grapes to 15 lbs (13½ lbs US; 6.9 kg): Grape & Apple (apples 4 lbs; 3¼ lbs US; 1.8 kg); Grape & Blackberry (blackberries 4 lbs; 3¼ lbs US; 1.8 kg); Grape & Damson (damsons 4 lbs; 3½ lbs US; 1.8 kg); Grape & Elderberry (elderberries 3 lbs; 2½ lbs US; 1.4 kg); Grape & Loganberry (loganberries 4 lbs; 3¼ lbs US; 1.8 kg); Grape & Mulberry (mulberries 4 lbs; 3¼ lbs US; 1.8 kg); Grape & Plum (plums 4 lbs; 3¼ lbs US; 1.8 kg); and Grape & Sloe (sloes 2 lbs; 1¾ lbs US; 905 g).

GRAPEFRUIT

A wine without much character, but pleasant enough and helped by the addition of sultanas to give it body. Avoid including the white pith and pips, which would give the wine an unpleasantly harsh taste.

	IMP	US	METRIC
large grapefruit	6	6	6
sugar	2 lbs	1¾ lbs	905 g
sultanas	1 lb	14 ozs	453 g
Camden tablet	1	1	1
pectin enzyme	1 tsp	1 tsp	1 tsp
water			
wine yeast			
yeast nutrient			

1. Cut the grapefruit in half and squeeze out the juice, leaving in any fruit pulp but discarding all pips.
2. Measure the juice and make up to 6 pints (3.4 l) with cold water.
3. Pare the rind thinly from 2 of the grapefruit, avoiding the white pith, and add to the liquid together with the crushed Camden tablet and pectin enzyme. Cover and leave for 24 hours.
4. Heat a further 2 pints (1.1 l) of water to boiling point and dissolve the sugar in it. When this syrup has cooled to blood heat, add it to the grapefruit pulp together with the yeast, nutrient and chopped sultanas. Cover well and leave in a warm place to ferment for 5–6 days, stirring twice daily.
5. Strain the liquid off the pulp and transfer to a fermenting jar. Fit bung and air-lock and leave to ferment on, racking when the wine begins clearing.
6. When all fermentation has ceased and the wine has cleared completely, bottle and store in a cool dark place to mature for at least 6 months.

GREENGAGE

These round green plums make a light white wine. They should be as ripe as possible, even over-ripe so long as they're sound.

	IMP	US	METRIC
ripe greengages	3 lbs	2½ lbs	1.4 kg
sugar	3½ lbs	3 lbs	1.6 kg
Camden tablet	1	1	1
pectin enzyme	2 tsps	2 tsps	2 tsps
water	1 gallon	1 gallon	4.5 l
wine yeast			
yeast nutrient			

1. Put the washed fruit into a vessel and crush, taking care not to break any stones. Cover with 6 pints (3.4 l) of cold water, stir in the Camden tablet and pectin enzyme, and leave to steep for 24 hours.
2. Heat a further 2 pints (1.1 l) of water to boiling point and dissolve the sugar in it.
3. When this syrup has cooled to blood heat, add it to the greengage pulp, followed by the yeast and nutrient.
4. Cover the vessel and leave in a warm place to ferment for 3 days, stirring twice daily.
5. Strain the liquid off the pulp and transfer to a fermenting jar. Fit an air-lock and leave to ferment on, racking when the wine begins to clear. When all fermentation has ceased and the wine is clear, bottle and store in a cool dark place to mature for at least 6 months.

LEMON

This is best made as a sweet wine because of the high acidity of the fruit. Avoid including any white pith or pips. This recipe can also be used to make lime wine.

	IMP	US	METRIC
ripe lemons	10	10	10
sugar	3 lbs	2½ lbs	1.4 kg
sultanas	1 lb	14 ozs	453 g
Camden tablet	1	1	1
water			
wine yeast			
yeast nutrient			

1. Cut the lemons in half and squeeze out the juice, leaving in any fruit pulp but discarding all pips.
2. Measure the juice and make up to 6 pints (3.4 l) with cold water.
3. Add the minced sultanas and the crushed Camden tablet, cover and leave to steep for 24 hours.
4. Bring a further 2 pints (1.1 l) of water to the boil and dissolve the sugar in it. Allow this syrup to cool, then add to the lemon liquid together with the yeast and nutrient.
5. Cover closely and keep in a warm place to ferment for 4 days, stirring twice daily.
6. Strain the liquid into a fermenting jar, fit an air-lock and leave to ferment on, racking when the wine starts to clear.
7. When all fermentation has finished and the wine is clear, bottle and store in a cool dark place to mature for at least 6 months.

MEDLAR

Medlars are small brown tree fruit related to apples and pears. The pleasantly astringent flavour doesn't appear until the fruit has begun to decay, so use medlars that are definitely over-ripe – this is the only exception to the rule not to use decaying material for wine-making.

	IMP	US	METRIC
medlars	8 lbs	7 lbs	3.6 kg
sugar	3 lbs	2½ lbs	1.4 kg
sultanas	8 ozs	7 ozs	226 g
Camden tablet	1	1	1
pectin enzyme	2 tsps	2 tsps	2 tsps
grape tannin	½ tsp	½ tsp	½ tsp
water	1 gallon	1 gallon	4.5 l
wine yeast			
yeast nutrient			

1. Put the medlars into a vessel, pulp them and cover with 6 pints (3.4 l) of cold water. Add the crushed Camden tablet and pectin enzyme and leave to steep overnight.

2. Heat a further 2 pints (1.1 l) of water to boiling point and dissolve the sugar in it. When this syrup has cooled to blood heat, add it to the medlar pulp together with the yeast, nutrient, tannin and chopped sultanas.

3. Cover closely and leave to ferment in a warm place for 3 days, stirring twice daily.

4. Strain the liquid off the pulp and transfer to a fermenting jar. Close off with an air-lock and leave to ferment on, racking when the wine starts to clear.

5. Once all fermentation has ceased and the wine has cleared completely, bottle and store in a cool dark place to mature for at least 6 months.

MELON

Wine from melon can be made with Demerara sugar to give a rich golden colour. This recipe can also be used to make wines from marrows and pumpkins.

	IMP	US	METRIC
ripe melon	5 lbs	4½ lbs	2.3 kg
sugar	3 lbs	2½ lbs	1.4 kg
lemons	2	2	2
root ginger	1 oz	$^7/_8$ oz	28 g
Camden tablet	1	1	1
pectin enzyme	1 tsp	1 tsp	1 tsp
water	1 gallon	1 gallon	4.5 l
wine yeast			
yeast nutrient			

1. Wash the melon, peel and remove the seeds and slice into a vessel, add the bruised ginger and cover with 6 pints (3.4 l) of cold water. Stir in the crushed Camden tablet and pectin enzyme and leave for 24 hours. Bring a further 2 pints (1.1 l) of water to the boil and in it dissolve the sugar. Cool to blood heat, then add to the melons together with the yeast and nutrient and the juice of the lemons.
2. Cover and keep in a warm place to ferment for 5 days, stirring twice daily. Strain the liquid carefully off the pulp and transfer to a fermenting jar.
3. Fit an air-lock and leave to ferment on, racking when the wine starts to clear.
4. When the fermentation has ended and the wine cleared, bottle and store in a cool dark place to mature for at least 6 months.

H. W. Buckbee

Rockford, Ill. U.S.A.

Seed and Plant Guide

1899

EXTRA EARLY
CHIEF CAULIFLOWE
PKT. 15¢

NEW
STRAWBERRY MUSK MELON
PKT. 10¢

BUCKBEE'S
SPOT CASH TOMATO
PKT. 10¢

Seeds
of
Prosperity

ORANGE

The best oranges to use are sweet, juicy and thin-skinned, and you'll need about 12 large ones for the required amount of orange juice. As with all citrus fruits, avoid including any white pith or pips. The addition of a little lemon juice helps the acidity of this wine.

	IMP	US	METRIC
fresh orange juice	2 pints	2 pints	1.1 l
sugar	3½ lbs	3 lbs	1.6 kg
lemons	2	2	2
Camden tablet	1	1	1
grape tannin	½ tsp	½ tsp	½ tsp
water			
wine yeast			
yeast nutrient			

1. Cut the oranges in half and use a lemon squeezer to press out 2 pints (1.1 l) of juice, removing any pips.
2. Make the juice up to 6 pints (3.4 l) with cold water.
3. Pare the rind very thinly from 4 of the oranges and add this to the juice. Stir in the crushed Camden tablet, cover and leave for 24 hours. Dissolve the sugar in 2 pints (1.1 l) of boiling water, cool, then add to the orange juice together with the yeast and nutrient, the grape tannin and the juice of the lemons.
4. Cover and leave to ferment in a warm place for 4 days, stirring twice daily. Strain the liquid into a fermenting jar, close off with an air-lock and leave to ferment on, racking when the wine begins to clear.
5. Once all fermentation has ended and the wine is completely clear, bottle and store in a cool dark place to mature for at least 6 months.

PEACH

Use fresh, well-ripened peaches – if the fruit isn't quite ripe it will leave an unpleasantly bitter taste in the wine.

	IMP	US	METRIC
ripe peaches	3 lbs	2½ lbs	1.4 kg
sugar	2½ lbs	2 lbs	1.2 kg
lemon	1	1	1
Camden tablet	1	1	1
pectin enzyme	2 tsps	2 tsps	2 tsps
water	1 gallon	1 gallon	4.5 l
wine yeast			
yeast nutrient			

1. Peel the peaches, remove the stones and crush the fruit. Cover the pulp with 6 pints (3.4 l) of cold water, stir in the crushed Camden tablet and pectin enzyme, and leave to steep for 24 hours.
2. Bring a further 2 pints (1.1 l) of water to the boil and dissolve the sugar in it.
3. Cool this syrup to blood heat, then add it to the peach pulp together with the yeast and nutrient and the juice of the lemon.
4. Cover closely and leave in a warm place to ferment for 4 days, stirring twice daily.
5. Strain the liquid off the pulp and transfer to a fermenting jar. Fit an air-lock and leave to ferment on, racking when the wine starts to clear. When all fermentation has ceased and the wine cleared, bottle and store in a cool dark place to mature for at least 6 months.

FROM A
Push-Cart
To a
Trolley-Car
IN
FRUIT GROWING

Crosby   Oldmixon   Elberta

HALE'S PEACHES
ALWAYS BEST IN MARKET

J.H. & J.H. Hale
137 acres

South Glastonbury
Connecticut
Hale Georgia Orchard Co.
887 acres
Fort Valley Georgia

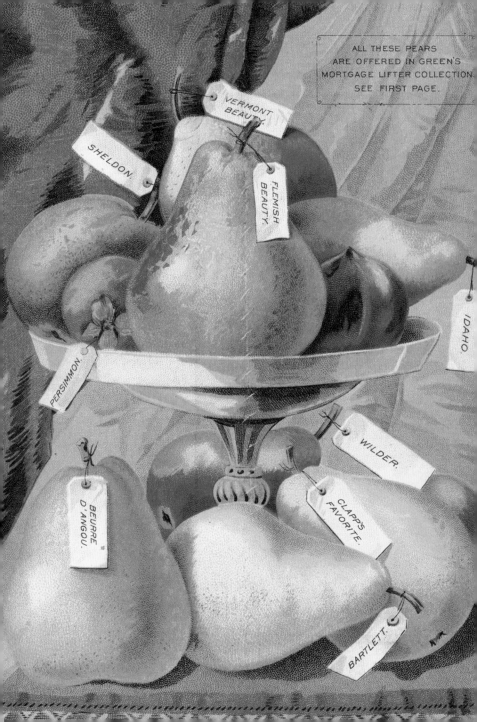

ALL THESE PEARS ARE OFFERED IN GREEN'S MORTGAGE LIFTER COLLECTION. SEE FIRST PAGE.

VERMONT BEAUTY.

SHELDON.

FLEMISH BEAUTY.

IDAHO.

PERSIMMON.

WILDER.

BEURRE D'ANGOU.

CLAPP'S FAVORITE.

BARTLETT.

PEAR

This is a difficult wine – it discolours easily and tends to lose its flavour and become vinegary. Contrary to the usual wine-making rule, don't attempt to use ripe fruit or the results will be disappointing. Choose pears that are fully grown but unripe – the variety doesn't matter.

	IMP	US	METRIC
pears	5 lbs	4½ lbs	2.3 kg
sugar	2½ lbs	2 lbs	1.2 kg
lemons	3	3	3
Camden tablets	2	2	2
pectin enzyme	1 tsp	1 tsp	1 tsp
water			
wine yeast			
yeast nutrient			

1. Put the pears through a fruit press or coarse mincer, collecting all the juice as it runs out.
2. Transfer the pulp and juice to a vessel and pour over 4 pints (2.25 l) of boiling water. When this has cooled, stir in the crushed Camden tablets and pectin enzyme, cover and leave for 24 hours.
3. Strain the liquid, pressing the pulp firmly to extract as much remaining juice as possible. Measure and make up to 1 gallon (4.5 l) with lukewarm water.
4. Stir in the sugar until it dissolves, then add the yeast, nutrient and juice of the lemons.
5. Cover well and keep in a warm place to ferment for 4 days, stirring twice daily.
6. Transfer to a fermenting jar, fit an air-lock and leave to ferment on, racking when the wine begins to clear.
7. Once all fermentation has ended and the wine is completely clear, bottle and store in a cool dark place to mature for at least 6 months.

PLUM

The colour of this very popular wine will depend on the variety of plum used: yellow plums give a pale golden colour, purple plums a deeper one, and Victoria plums (the best kind to use) produce a lovely rosé.

	IMP	US	METRIC
ripe plums	4 lbs	3¼ lbs	1.8 kg
sugar	3 lbs	2½ lbs	1.4 kg
sultanas	8 ozs	7 ozs	226 g
lemon	1	1	1
Camden tablets	2	2	2
pectin enzyme	2 tsps	2 tsps	2 tsps
water	7 pints	7 pints	4 l
wine yeast			
yeast nutrient			

1. Halve the plums, remove the stones and crush the fruit well. Cover with 5 pints (2.8 l) of cold water, add the Camden tablets and pectin enzyme, and leave to steep for 24 hours.
2. Bring a further 2 pints (1.1 l) of water to the boil and dissolve the sugar in it. Let this syrup cool to blood heat, then add to the plum pulp together with the yeast and nutrient, the minced sultanas and juice of the lemon. Cover and leave in a warm place to ferment for 4 days, stirring twice daily. Strain the liquid off the pulp, measure it and if necessary make up to 1 gallon (4.5 l) with cool boiled water.
3. Transfer to a fermenting jar, close off with bung and air-lock and leave to ferment on, racking when the wine starts to clear.
4. When all fermentation has ceased and the wine has cleared, bottle and store in a cool dark place to mature for at least 6 months, preferably a little longer.

QUINCE

The fruit of the ornamental quince, or japonica, is the best to use since it contains less acid than the other varieties. Gather the ripe quinces in early autumn when they've turned golden yellow and give off a distinctive fragrance.

	IMP	US	METRIC
ripe quinces	4 lbs	3¼ lbs	1.8 kg
sugar	2½ lbs	2 lbs	1.2 kg
sultanas	1 lb	14 ozs	453 g
lemons	2	2	2
Camden tablets	2	2	2
pectin enzyme	2 tsps	2 tsps	2 tsps
water	1 gallon	1 gallon	4.5 l
wine yeast			
yeast nutrient			

1. Cut up or grate the quinces finely, taking care not to include any core.
2. Put them into a vessel and cover with 6 pints (3.4 l) of boiling water and when this has cooled, stir in the crushed Camden tablets and pectin enzyme.
3. Cover and leave to steep for 48 hours, stirring occasionally.
4. Strain the liquid from the pulp, pressing well to extract the juice.
5. Heat a further 2 pints (1.1 l) of water to boiling point and dissolve the sugar in it. Cool, then add to the quince liquid together with the yeast and nutrient, the chopped sultanas and the juice of the lemons.
6. Cover well and leave to ferment in a warm place for 4 days, stirring twice daily.
7. Strain into a fermenting jar, fit an air-lock and leave to ferment on, racking when the wine starts to clear.
8. When the fermentation has finished and the wine cleared, bottle and store in a cool dark place to mature for at least 6 months.

RHUBARB

Rhubarb contains semi-poisonous oxalic acid, which must be removed before the wine is made. This is easily done with the aid of precipitated chalk – available from chemists or drug stores. Rhubarb wine tends to be uninteresting by itself, but blends very well with other wines and is worth making for that purpose. For best results, use fresh young stalks, preferably red ones.

	IMP	US	METRIC
rhubarb stalks	5 lbs	4½ lbs	2.3 kg
sugar	3 lbs	2½ lbs	1.4 kg
raisins	1 lb	14 ozs	453 g
lemons	3	3	3
Camden tablet	1	1	1
grape tannin	½ tsp	½ tsp	½ tsp
precipitated chalk	1 oz	$^7/_8$ oz	28 g
water			
wine yeast			
yeast nutrient			

1. Wash the rhubarb stalks and cut them in short lengths into a vessel. Crush well, using a mallet or similar wooden implement.
2. Cover with 6 pints (3.4 l) of cold water, add the crushed Camden tablet and leave to steep for 48 hours, stirring occasionally.
3. Strain off the liquid, pressing the pulp well to extract as much juice as possible.
4. Stir in the precipitated chalk – the liquid will fizz vigorously. Continue stirring until the fizzing subsides, then leave the liquid undisturbed until the chalk has settled to the bottom.
5. Siphon the cleared liquid off the chalk deposit. Measure and if necessary make back up to 6 pints (3.4 l) with cool boiled water.

6. Heat a further 2 pints (1.1 l) of water to boiling point and dissolve the sugar in it. When this syrup has cooled add it to the rhubarb liquid together with the yeast and nutrient, the grape tannin, chopped raisins and juice of the lemons.
7. Cover well and leave in a warm place to ferment for 5 days, stirring twice daily.
8. Strain the liquid into a fermenting jar, close off with bung and airlock and leave to ferment on, racking when the wine begins to clear.
9. Once all fermentation has ceased and the wine cleared, bottle and store in a cool dark place to mature for at least 6 months.

GRAIN
WINES

BARLEY

Wines made from grain – wheat, barley, rye, maize and rice – are cheap and easy to produce, and look rather like whisky or brandy. It's most important that they are left in bottles to mature for at least a year – drunk too soon they do no justice to themselves, and, worse, can give you a powerful hangover. Use a special cereal wine yeast which will help prevent too much starch haze, and select only clean, uncontaminated grain. All grain wines are produced by the same method, using either white or Demerara sugar, and are best made medium sweet or sweet.

	IMP	US	METRIC
pearl barley	1 lb	14 ozs	453 g
sugar	3½ lbs	3 lbs	1.6 kg
raisins	1 lb	14 ozs	453 g
lemons	2	2	2
large old potatoes	2	2	2
grape tannin	1 tsp	1 tsp	1 tsp
water	1 gallon	1 gallon	4.5 l
cereal wine yeast			
yeast nutrient			

1. Put the grain, chopped raisins and the scrubbed and sliced potatoes into a fermenting vessel.
2. Bring 1 gallon (4.5 l) of water to the boil and stir in the sugar until dissolved.
3. Pour over the grain, leave until just comfortably warm, then stir in the yeast and nutrient, the grape tannin and the juice of the citrus fruit. Cover closely and leave in a warm place to ferment for 10 days, stirring twice daily.

4. Strain the liquid off the pulp and transfer to a fermenting jar. Fit bung and air-lock and leave to ferment on, racking when the wine begins to clear.
5. When all fermentation has ceased and the wine is brilliantly clear, bottle and store in a cool dark place to mature for at least a year, preferably longer.

MAIZE (OR CORN)

All grain wines are produced by the same method, using either white or Demerara sugar, and are best made medium sweet or sweet.

	IMP	US	METRIC
crushed maize	1 lb	14 ozs	453 g
sugar	3 lbs	2½ lbs	1.4 kg
raisins	1 lb	14 ozs	453 g
lemon	1	1	1
oranges	3	3	3
grape tannin	1 tsp	1 tsp	1 tsp
water	1 gallon	1 gallon	4.5 l
cereal wine yeast			
yeast nutrient			

1. Put the grain and chopped raisins into a fermenting vessel.
2. Bring 1 gallon (4.5 l) of water to the boil and stir in the sugar until dissolved.
3. Pour over the grain, leave until just comfortably warm, then stir in the yeast and nutrient, the grape tannin and the juice of the citrus fruit. Cover closely and leave in a warm place to ferment for 10 days, stirring twice daily.
4. Strain the liquid off the pulp and transfer to a fermenting jar. Fit bung and air-lock and leave to ferment on, racking when the wine begins to clear.
5. When all fermentation has ceased and the wine is brilliantly clear, bottle and store in a cool dark place to mature for at least a year, preferably longer.

WE ARE THE
PIONEERS

NO. 2.

NO. 1. WILL'S GEHU 70 DAY FLINT CORN
NO. 2 WILL'S PIONEER WHITE DENT CORN
NO. 3. WILL'S NORTHWESTERN DENT CORN
THE EARLIEST DENT CORN ON EARTH

RICE

All grain wines are produced by the same method, using either white or Demerara sugar, and are best made medium sweet or sweet.

	IMP	US	METRIC
patna rice	3 lbs	2½ lbs	1.4 kg
sugar	3 lbs	2½ lbs	1.4 kg
raisins	1 lb	14 ozs	453 g
lemon	1	1	1
oranges	2	2	2
grape tannin	1 tsp	1 tsp	1 tsp
water	1 gallon	1 gallon	4.5 l
cereal wine yeast			
yeast nutrient			

1. Put the grain and chopped raisins into a fermenting vessel.
2. Bring 1 gallon (4.5 l) of water to the boil and stir in the sugar until dissolved.
3. Pour over the grain, leave until just comfortably warm, then stir in the yeast and nutrient, the grape tannin and the juice of the citrus fruit. Cover closely and leave in a warm place to ferment for 10 days, stirring twice daily.
4. Strain the liquid off the pulp and transfer to a fermenting jar. Fit bung and air-lock and leave to ferment on, racking when the wine begins to clear.
5. When all fermentation has ceased and the wine is brilliantly clear, bottle and store in a cool dark place to mature for at least a year, preferably longer.

RYE

All grain wines are produced by the same method, using either white or Demerara sugar, and are best made medium sweet or sweet.

	IMP	US	METRIC
rye	2 lbs	1¾ lbs	905 g
sugar	3 lbs	2½ lbs	1.4 kg
raisins	1 lb	14 ozs	453 g
lemons	2	2	2
grape tannin	1 tsp	1 tsp	1 tsp
water	1 gallon	1 gallon	4.5 l
cereal wine yeast			
yeast nutrient			

1. Put the grain and chopped raisins into a fermenting vessel.
2. Bring 1 gallon (4.5 l) of water to the boil and stir in the sugar until dissolved.
3. Pour over the grain, leave until just comfortably warm, then stir in the yeast and nutrient, the grape tannin and the juice of the citrus fruit. Cover closely and leave in a warm place to ferment for 10 days, stirring twice daily.
4. Strain the liquid off the pulp and transfer to a fermenting jar. Fit bung and air-lock and leave to ferment on, racking when the wine begins to clear.
5. When all fermentation has ceased and the wine is brilliantly clear, bottle and store in a cool dark place to mature for at least a year, preferably longer.

THIS 100 ACRES WILL YIELD 8000 BUSHELS SURE.

SALZER'S RED ✠ CROSS ✠ WINTER W.

PRICE
BU... $1⁶⁵
½ BUS. $4⁰⁰
0 BUS.. $14⁰⁰

PRIC
1 BU.. S
2½ BUS.
10 BUS.

SEND ALL ORDERS
TO
JOHN A. SALZER SEED Cᴼ LA CROSSE WIS

WHEAT

All grain wines are produced by the same method, using either white or Demerara sugar, and are best made medium sweet or sweet.

	IMP	US	METRIC
wheat	2 lbs	1¾ lbs	905 g
sugar	3 lbs	2½ lbs	1.4 kg
raisins	2 lbs	1¾ lbs	905 g
lemons	2	2	2
grape tannin	1 tsp	1 tsp	1 tsp
water	1 gallon	1 gallon	4.5 l
cereal wine yeast			
yeast nutrient			

1. Put the grain and chopped raisins into a fermenting vessel.
2. Bring 1 gallon (4.5 l) of water to the boil and stir in the sugar until dissolved.
3. Pour over the grain, leave until just comfortably warm, then stir in the yeast and nutrient, the grape tannin and the juice of the citrus fruit. Cover closely and leave in a warm place to ferment for 10 days, stirring twice daily.
4. Strain the liquid off the pulp and transfer to a fermenting jar. Fit bung and air-lock and leave to ferment on, racking when the wine begins to clear.
5. When all fermentation has ceased and the wine is brilliantly clear, bottle and store in a cool dark place to mature for at least a year, preferably longer.

HERB WINES

BALM

This herb is often called lemon balm because of its distinctive aroma. The wine is best made from the tender tips of mature plants.

	IMP	US	METRIC
balm tips	4 pints	4 pints	2.25 l
sugar	2½ lbs	2 lbs	1.2 kg
lemons	2	2	2
Camden tablet	1	1	1
water	1 gallon	1 gallon	4.5 l
wine yeast			
yeast nutrient			

1. Bruise the balm tips and cover with 6 pints (3.4 l) of boiling water.
2. Stir in the crushed Camden tablet, cover and leave to infuse for 24 hours. Strain the liquid, pressing the pulp well.
3. Heat a further 2 pints (1.1 l) of water to boiling point and dissolve the sugar in it. When this syrup has cooled to blood heat, add it to the balm liquid, followed by the yeast, nutrient and juice of the lemons.
4. Cover well and leave in a warm place to ferment for 3 days, stirring twice daily.
5. Transfer to a fermenting jar, close off with an air-lock and leave to ferment on, racking when the wine starts to clear.
6. When all fermentation has ended and the wine has cleared, bottle and store in a cool dark place to mature for at least 6 months.

MINT

This herb comes in several varieties, including spearmint, lemon mint and apple mint. All are suitable for wine-making, though spearmint will give a stronger flavour.

	IMP	US	METRIC
mint leaves	1½ pints	1½ pints	852 ml
sugar	3 lbs	2½ lbs	1.4 kg
sultanas	8 ozs	7 ozs	226 g
lemons	2	2	2
Camden tablet	1	1	1
grape tannin	½ tsp	½ tsp	½ tsp
water	1 gallon	1 gallon	4.5 l
wine yeast			
yeast nutrient			

1. Bruise the mint leaves in a vessel and cover with 1 gallon (4.5 l) of boiling water. Stir in the crushed Camden tablet, cover and leave to infuse for 24 hours.
2. Strain off the liquid, pressing the pulp well.
3. Draw off 2 pints (1.1 l) of the mint liquid, bring just to boiling point and in it dissolve the sugar.
4. Allow this syrup to cool, then return to the bulk of the liquid and add the yeast and nutrient, the chopped sultanas, grape tannin and juice of the lemons.
5. Cover well and leave in a warm place to ferment for 4 days, stirring twice daily.
6. Strain into a fermenting jar, fit an air-lock and leave to ferment on, racking when the wine is clearing.
7. When all fermentation has ceased and the wine cleared completely, bottle and store in a cool dark place to mature for at least 6 months.

NETTLE

Use the tips of the nettles only and pick them in late spring when they're young and juicy, to make a pale golden wine.

	IMP	US	METRIC
nettle tips	4 pints	4 pints	2.25 l
sugar	3 lbs	2½ lbs	1.4 kg
lemons	2	2	2
root ginger	½ oz	½ oz	14 g
Camden tablet	1	1	1
water	1 gallon	1 gallon	4.5 l
wine yeast			
yeast nutrient			

1. Crush the Camden tablet in 1 gallon (4.5 l) of cold water and soak the nettle tips in this for 24 hours.
2. Add the bruised ginger, bring all to the boil and simmer gently for 15–20 minutes.
3. Strain the liquid on to the sugar and stir until dissolved.
4. Leave until the liquid is comfortably warm, then add the yeast, nutrient and juice of the lemons.
5. Cover well and keep in a warm place to ferment for 5 days, stirring twice daily.
6. Transfer to a fermenting jar, close off with an air-lock and leave to ferment on, racking when the wine starts clearing.
7. When all fermentation has stopped and the wine cleared, bottle and store in a cool dark place to mature for at least 6 months.

PARSLEY

This is one of the most popular home-made wines. Two varieties can be made – one early in the year from the dark green leaves, the other in summer from the younger, fresh green leaves. The stalks have too strong a flavour, so avoid including them.

	IMP	US	METRIC
fresh parsley leaves	1 lb	14 ozs	453 g
sugar	2½ lbs	2 lbs	1.2 kg
sultanas	8 ozs	7 ozs	226 g
lemons	2	2	2
oranges	2	2	2
Camden tablet	1	1	1
grape tannin	½ tsp	½ tsp	½ tsp
water	1 gallon	1 gallon	4.5 l
wine yeast			
yeast nutrient			

1. Put the washed parsley into a vessel and cover with 1 gallon (4.5 l) of boiling water. Stir in the crushed Camden tablet, cover and leave to infuse for 24 hours.
2. Strain the liquid off and discard the pulp.
3. Draw off 2 pints (1.1 l) of the liquid and bring just to the boil. Dissolve the sugar thoroughly in this, cool to blood heat, then return to the bulk of the liquid, followed by the yeast and nutrient, the chopped sultanas, grape tannin and juice of the citrus fruits.
4. Cover well and leave to ferment in a warm place for 4 days, stirring twice daily.
5. Strain into a fermenting jar, fit bung and air-lock and leave to ferment on, racking when the wine is beginning to clear.
6. When all fermentation has ceased and the wine is quite clear, bottle and store in a cool dark place to mature for at least 6 months.

THYME

There are three varieties of thyme – lemon, orange and caraway – each with its own special flavour. For wine-making purposes, lemon thyme is best. Strip the leaves from the stalks before using.

	IMP	US	METRIC
thyme leaves	2 pints	2 pints	1.1 l
sugar	2½ lbs	2 lbs	1.2 kg
sultanas	8 ozs	7 ozs	226 g
lemons	2	2	2
Camden tablet	1	1	1
water	1 gallon	1 gallon	4.5 l
wine yeast			
yeast nutrient			

1. Bruise the leaves in a vessel and cover them with 1 gallon (4.5 l) of boiling water. Stir in the crushed Camden tablet and leave to infuse for 24 hours. Strain off the liquid and discard the pulp.
2. Bring 2 pints (1.1 l) of the liquid to boiling point and in it dissolve the sugar.
3. Cool slightly before returning to the bulk of the liquid, then add the yeast and nutrient, the chopped sultanas and juice of the lemons.
4. Cover and leave in a warm place to ferment for 4 days, stirring twice daily.
5. Strain into a fermenting jar, close off with an air-lock and leave to ferment on, racking when the wine starts to clear.
6. When all fermentation has ended and the wine cleared, bottle and store in a cool dark place to mature for at least 6 months.

LEAF AND
SAP WINES

BIRCH SAP

Birch sap wine was introduced into England from the Baltic and is one of the oldest country wines. Writing in 1718, Ned Ward, author of *The London Spy*, described it as 'Wine drawn out of a Birch Tree ... drinks almost like Mead, and makes a man's mouth smell of Honey'. The sap should be collected when it is rising, early in March, from a mature tree. Bore a hole to a depth of 1½ inches (38 mm), large enough to take a piece of plastic tubing. The hole should be slanted at an angle of 45° and sited between 18–24 inches (457–610 mm) from the ground. Secure the other end of the tubing in a clean container and leave until 1 gallon (4.5 l) of sap has been collected – generally a couple of days. Remove the tubing from the tree, being careful to stop up the hole tightly with a wooden plug or cork to prevent more sap oozing out. To avoid harming the tree, don't tap it more than once every two years, and don't take more than 1 gallon (4.5 l) at a time. Wines from sycamore sap and walnut sap can also be made to this recipe.

	IMP	US	METRIC
birch sap	1 gallon	1 gallon	4.5 l
sugar	2½ lbs	2 lbs	1.2 kg
raisins	8 ozs	7 ozs	226 g
lemons	2	2	2
orange	1	1	1
grape tannin	1 tsp	1 tsp	1 tsp
wine yeast			
yeast nutrient			

1. Boil the sap, sugar and chopped raisins together for 10 minutes.
2. Leave until comfortably warm, then stir in the yeast and nutrient, the grape tannin and juice of the citrus fruits.

3. Cover well and leave to ferment in a warm place for 4–5 days, stirring twice daily.
4. Strain into a fermenting jar, fit bung and air-lock and leave to ferment on, racking when the wine starts to clear.
5. When the fermentation has ended and the wine completely cleared, bottle and store in a cool dark place to mature for at least 6 months.

FOLLY (OR VINE PRUNINGS)

Folly (from the French *feuillage*: 'in leaf') is made from the summer prunings of the grape vine, using the leaves, tendrils and green shoots.

	IMP	US	METRIC
grape vine prunings	4 lbs	3¼ lbs	1.8 kg
sugar	2½ lbs	2 lbs	1.2 kg
lemons	2	2	2
Camden tablet	1	1	1
water	1 gallon	1 gallon	4.5 l
wine yeast			
yeast nutrient			

1. Put the washed prunings into a vessel and cover with 6 pints (3.4 l) of boiling water. Stir in the crushed Camden tablet and leave to infuse for 48 hours, stirring occasionally to submerge the top leaves.
2. Strain the liquid off and discard the prunings.
3. Bring a further 2 pints (1.1 l) of water to the boil and in it dissolve the sugar. When this syrup has cooled to blood heat, add it to the prunings liquid, followed by the yeast, nutrient and juice of the lemons.
4. Cover well and leave to ferment in a warm place for 4 days, stirring twice daily.
5. Transfer to a fermenting jar, fit an air-lock and leave to ferment on, racking when the wine begins clearing.
6. Once all fermentation has ended and the wine has cleared, bottle and store in a cool dark place to mature for at least 6 months.

OAK LEAF

Two varieties of this surprisingly good wine can be made – one at the end of June when the leaves are fully grown, the other in autumn when they're just turning brown. The leaves contain a lot of tannin, so don't overdo the amount used or the wine will be too astringent. This recipe can also be used to make walnut leaf wine.

	IMP	US	METRIC
oak leaves	4 pints	4 pints	2.25 l
sugar	3 lbs	2½ lbs	1.4 kg
sultanas	8 ozs	7 ozs	226 g
lemons	2	2	2
orange	1	1	1
Camden tablet	1	1	1
water	1 gallon	1 gallon	4.5 l
wine yeast			
yeast nutrient			

1. Wash the leaves well, put them into a vessel and cover them with 1 gallon (4.5 l) of boiling water. Stir in the crushed Camden tablet, cover and leave to infuse for 24 hours.
2. Strain the liquid from the leaves, bring it just to boiling point and stir in the sugar until dissolved.
3. Leave until comfortably warm, then add the yeast and nutrient, the chopped sultanas and juice of the citrus fruits.
4. Cover and leave to ferment in a warm place for 4 days, stirring twice daily. Strain into a fermenting jar, close off with an air-lock and leave to ferment on, racking when the wine starts clearing.
5. When all fermentation has ceased and the wine cleared, bottle and store in a cool dark place to mature for at least 6 months.

VEGETABLE WINES

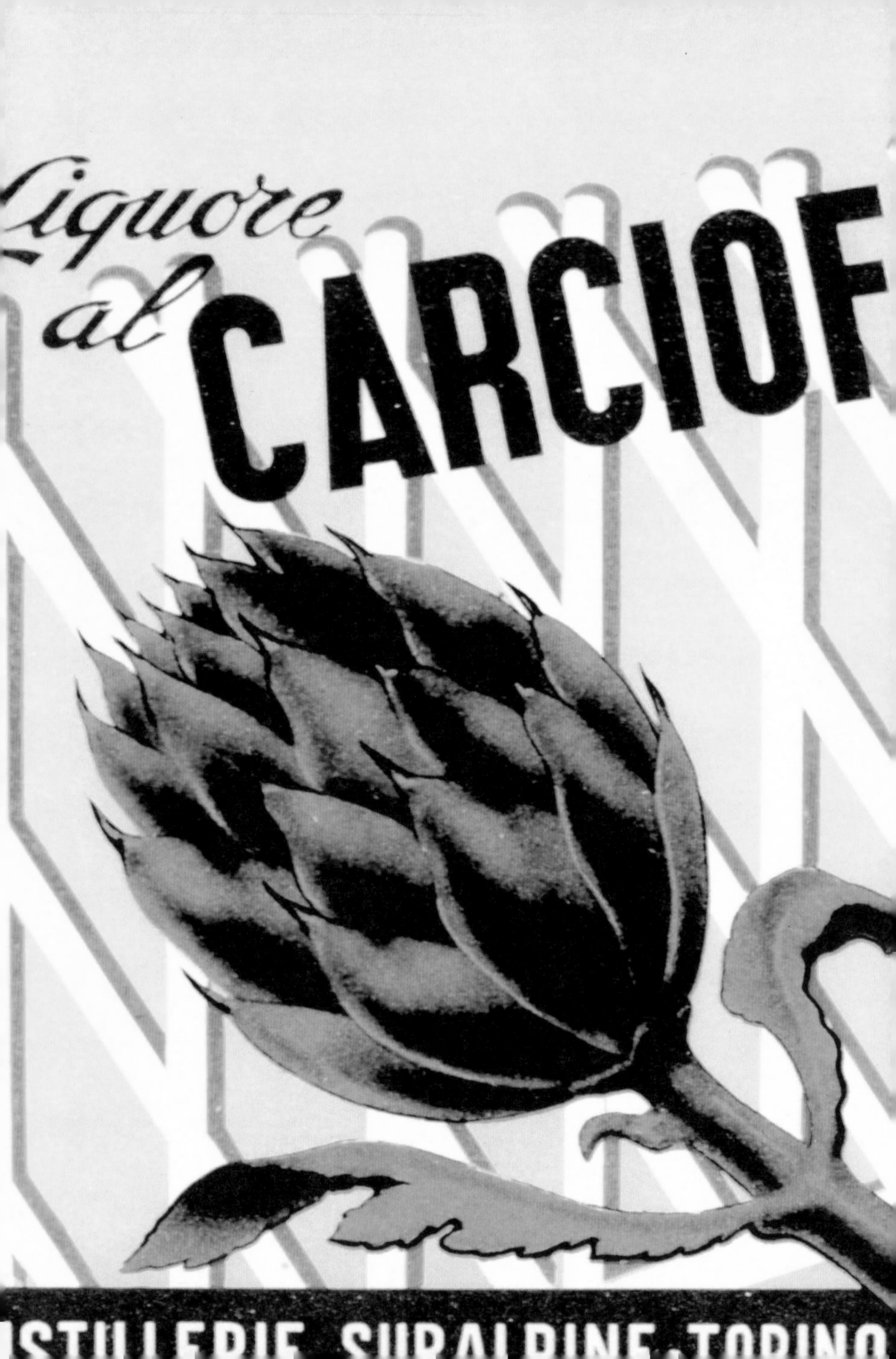
Liquore
al
CARCIOF
ISTILLERIE SUBALPINE TORINO

ARTICHOKE

Use Jerusalem, not globe, artichokes for this recipe. The Jerusalem is a member of the sunflower family – the name comes from the Italian girasole: sunflower – and it's often called a sunchoke in the USA.

	IMP	US	METRIC
artichokes	4 lbs	3¼ lbs	1.8 kg
sugar	2½ lbs	2 lbs	1.2 kg
sultanas	8 ozs	7 ozs	226 g
root ginger	1 oz	7/8 oz	28 g
lemon	1	1	1
orange	1	1	1
Camden tablet	1	1	1
water	1 gallon	1 gallon	4.5 l
wine yeast			
yeast nutrient			

1. Wash and slice the artichokes and add them to 1 gallon (4.5 l) of cold water together with the bruised ginger. Stir in the crushed Camden tablet, cover and leave for 24 hours.
2. Pare the rind of the citrus fruit very thinly, avoiding any white pith, and add this to the liquid.
3. Bring all to the boil and simmer for 30 minutes.
4. Strain the liquid over the sugar, stirring until dissolved. Leave until comfortably warm, then add the yeast and nutrient, the chopped sultanas and the juice of the citrus fruits.
5. Cover well and leave to ferment in a warm place for 3 days, stirring twice daily.
6. Strain into a fermenting jar, close off with bung and air-lock and leave to ferment on, racking when the wine begins clearing.
7. When all fermentation has ended and the wine cleared, bottle and store in a cool dark place to mature for at least 6 months, preferably 9 months.

AUBERGINE (OR EGGPLANT)

Aubergine (also known as eggplant) is one of the less common home-made wines, but worth making if only for its curiosity value. White or purple varieties can be used for this recipe.

	IMP	US	METRIC
ripe aubergines	3 lbs	2½ lbs	1.4 kg
sugar	2½ lbs	2 lbs	1.2 kg
lemons	2	2	2
orange juice	1 pint	1 pint	568 ml
Camden tablet	1	1	1
grape tannin	½ tsp	½ tsp	½ tsp
water	7 pints	7 pints	4 l
wine yeast			
yeast nutrient			

1. Peel and slice the aubergines into 7 pints (4 l) of cold water, stir in the crushed Camden tablet, and leave to steep for 24 hours.
2. Pare the rind very thinly from one of the lemons (avoiding all white pith) and add to the aubergines. Bring all to the boil and simmer until the aubergines are just soft, but not mushy.
3. Strain the liquid over the sugar and stir well until dissolved.
4. Leave until comfortably warm, then add the yeast and nutrient, the grape tannin and juice of the lemons, and a pint (568 ml) of fresh orange juice. Cover and leave in a warm place to ferment for 2 days, stirring twice daily. Strain into a fermenting jar, close off with an air-lock and leave to ferment on, racking when the wine starts to clear.
5. When all fermentation has ceased and the wine is quite clear, bottle and store in a cool dark place to mature for at least 6 months.

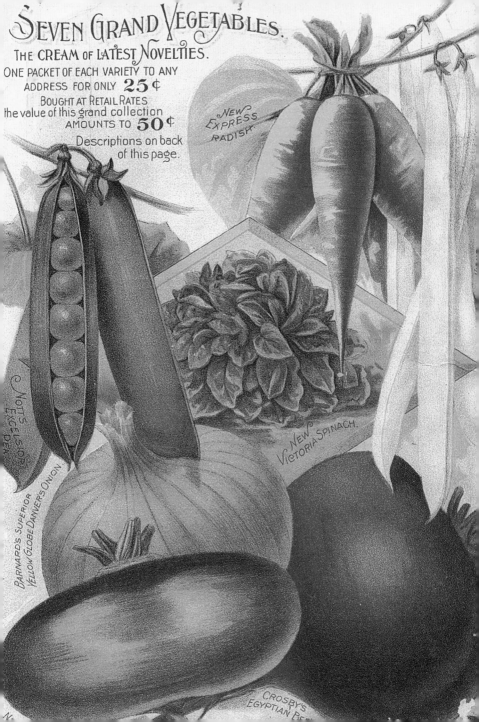

SEVEN GRAND VEGETABLES.

THE CREAM OF LATEST NOVELTIES.

ONE PACKET OF EACH VARIETY TO ANY
ADDRESS FOR ONLY **25**¢

BOUGHT AT RETAIL RATES
the value of this grand collection
AMOUNTS TO **50**¢

Descriptions on back
of this page.

NEW EXPRESS RADISH.

NEW VICTORIA SPINACH.

NOTT'S EXCELSIOR PEA.

BARNARD'S SUPERIOR YELLOW GLOBE DANVERS ONION.

CROSBY'S EGYPTIAN BEET

BEETROOT

Young juicy beets are no good for this wine – you need old, shrivelled ones with less starch and less earthy flavour. Too much light during the secondary fermentation will rob the wine of its rich jewel colour and turn it drab brown, so ferment it in a dark glass jar, or else cover a clear jar with a sleeve of brown paper.

	IMP	US	METRIC
old beetroots	4 lbs	3¼ lbs	1.8 kg
sugar	3 lbs	2½ lbs	1.4 kg
lemons	2	2	2
oranges	2	2	2
water			
wine yeast			
yeast nutrient			

1. Wash the beets well, without peeling, and slice them into sufficient water to cover them. Bring to the boil and simmer gently for 15 minutes.
2. Strain the liquid, measure and make up to 1 gallon (4.5 l) with boiling water. Stir in the sugar until dissolved.
3. When the liquid is comfortably warm, add the yeast, nutrient and juice of the citrus fruits.
4. Cover and leave in a warm place to ferment for 5 days, stirring twice daily. Transfer to a fermenting jar, close off with an air-lock and leave to ferment on, racking when the wine starts to clear.
5. Once all fermentation has ceased and the wine is brilliantly clear, bottle and store in a cool dark place. Beetroot wine takes longer than usual to mature, and is best left for at least 18 months.

BROAD BEAN

Old beans are best for this light, dry wine. Take great care not to let the skins split during the boiling process, or the starch released will make the wine hazy and difficult to clear. This recipe can also be used to make wine from fresh lima beans.

	IMP	US	METRIC
broad beans (shelled)	4 lbs	3¼ lbs	1.8 kg
sugar	2½ lbs	2 lbs	1.2 kg
raisins	8 ozs	7 ozs	226 g
lemons	2	2	2
water	1 gallon	1 gallon	4.5 l
wine yeast			
yeast nutrient			

1. Add the shelled beans to 1 gallon (4.5 l) of water, bring to the boil, cover and simmer very gently for 1 hour.
2. Strain the liquid off the beans, measure and if necessary make back up to the original volume.
3. Stir in the sugar, and when the liquid is just comfortably warm, add the yeast and nutrient, the chopped raisins and the juice of the lemons.
4. Cover closely and leave to ferment in a warm place for 4–5 days, stirring twice daily.
5. Strain into a fermenting jar, fit bung and air-lock and leave to ferment on, racking when the wine begins to clear.
6. When all fermentation has ceased and the wine has cleared, bottle and store in a cool dark place to mature for at least 6 months, preferably a year.

H.W. Buckbee

ROCKFORD, ILL. U.S.A.

SEEDS OF PROSPERITY.

898

BUCKBEE'S NEW GOLDEN LIMA

SEED AND PLANT GUIDE

CARROT

The best carrot wine is made from old roots and is rather like a dry sherry. Being a naturally sweet vegetable, it doesn't need a lot of sugar.

	IMP	US	METRIC
old carrots	4 lbs	3¼ lbs	1.8 kg
sugar	2½ lbs	2 lbs	1.2 kg
raisins	4 ozs	3½ ozs	113 g
root ginger	1 oz	⁷/₈ oz	28 g
lemons	2	2	2
grape tannin	½ tsp	½ tsp	½ tsp
water	1 gallon	1 gallon	4.5 l
wine yeast			
yeast nutrient			

1. Wash and slice the carrots, without peeling, and add to 1 gallon (4.5 l) of water with the bruised ginger.
2. Bring to the boil and simmer until just tender.
3. Discard the carrots, strain the liquid over the sugar and stir until dissolved.
4. When the liquid is comfortably warm, add the yeast and nutrient, the grape tannin, chopped raisins and juice of the lemons.
5. Cover and leave to ferment in a warm place for 8–9 days, stirring twice daily.
6. Strain into a fermenting jar, close off with an air-lock and leave to ferment on, racking when the wine is clearing.
7. When fermentation has ended and the wine cleared, bottle and store in a cool dark place to mature for at least 8 months, preferably 1 year.

CELERY

The green parts of the celery will give a bitter taste, so use only the white stalks and the heart, or root. The colour of the wine will depend on the sugar used – white sugar produces a white wine, Demerara a warm golden one.

	IMP	US	METRIC
celery	4 lbs	3¼ lbs	1.8 kg
sugar	3 lbs	2½ lbs	1.4 kg
lemons	2	2	2
water	1 gallon	1 gallon	4.5 l
wine yeast			
yeast nutrient			

1. Wash the celery, discarding any discoloured parts, and slice into 1 gallon (4.5 l) of boiling water.
2. Simmer until just tender, discard the celery and strain the liquid over the sugar, dissolving thoroughly.
3. Leave the liquid until comfortably warm, then add the yeast and nutrient and the juice of the lemons.
4. Keep well covered in a warm place to ferment for 4 days, stirring twice daily.
5. Transfer to a fermenting jar, close off with bung and air-lock and leave to ferment on, racking when the wine starts to clear.
6. When all fermentation has ceased and the wine cleared, bottle and store in a cool dark place to mature for at least 6 months.

LETTUCE

Not an outstanding wine, but a worthwhile way to use up a glut of lettuces. Avoid the 'white milk' found in the stem, which would give the wine a bitter taste. An attractively coloured spinach wine can be made with this recipe.

	IMP	US	METRIC
lettuce leaves	2½ lbs	2 lbs	1.2 kg
sugar	3 lbs	2½ lbs	1.4 kg
sultanas	8 ozs	7 ozs	226 g
lemons	2	2	2
water	1 gallon	1 gallon	4.5 l
wine yeast			
yeast nutrient			

1. Bring 1 gallon (4.5 l) of water to the boil, add the shredded lettuce leaves and simmer gently for 20 minutes.
2. Strain the liquid on to the sugar and stir until dissolved.
3. When the liquid is just comfortably warm, add the yeast and nutrient, the chopped sultanas and the juice of the lemons.
4. Keep covered in a warm place to ferment for 4 days, stirring twice daily. Strain into a fermenting jar, fit an air-lock and leave to ferment on, racking when the wine begins clearing.
5. When all fermentation has ceased and the wine cleared completely, bottle and store in a cool dark place to mature for at least 6 months.

MANGOLD

This is one of the oldest of the country wines and still a great favourite. If you don't grow mangolds yourself, they're easily obtainable from farms, where they're used as winter food for livestock. Mangolds are also known as mangel wurzels, sugar beet and mangel beet.

	IMP	US	METRIC
mangolds	5 lbs	4¼ lbs	2.3 kg
sugar	3 lbs	2½ lbs	1.4 kg
lemons	2	2	2
Camden tablet	1	1	1
pectin enzyme	1 tsp	1 tsp	1 tsp
grape tannin	½ tsp	½ tsp	½ tsp
water	1 gallon	1 gallon	4.5 l
wine yeast			
yeast nutrient			

1. Scrub the mangolds well, without peeling, and slice into 1 gallon (4.5 l) of cold water. Add the crushed Camden tablet and pectin enzyme and leave for 24 hours.
2. Bring to the boil and simmer gently until just tender. Strain off the liquid – don't press or wring the pulp – and pour over the sugar, stirring well.
3. Leave until comfortably warm, then add the yeast and nutrient, the grape tannin and juice of the lemons.
4. Cover and keep in a warm place to ferment for 5 days, stirring twice daily. Transfer to a fermenting jar, close off with an air-lock and leave to ferment on, racking when the wine begins to clear.
5. When all fermentation has ended and the wine is clear, bottle and store in a cool dark place to mature for at least 6 months, preferably 9 months.

MARROW (OR SQUASH)

Wine from marrows – called squashes in the USA – can be made with Demerara sugar to give a rich golden colour. This recipe can also be used to make wines from melons and pumpkins.

	IMP	US	METRIC
ripe marrows	5 lbs	4½ lbs	2.3 kg
sugar	3 lbs	2½ lbs	1.4 kg
lemons	2	2	2
root ginger	1 oz	⁷/₈ oz	28 g
Camden tablet	1	1	1
pectin enzyme	1 tsp	1 tsp	1 tsp
water	1 gallon	1 gallon	4.5 l
wine yeast			
yeast nutrient			

1. Wash the marrows, peel and slice them (with the seeds) into a vessel, add the bruised ginger and cover with 6 pints (3.4 l) of cold water. Stir in the crushed Camden tablet and pectin enzyme and leave for 24 hours. Bring a further 2 pints (1.1 l) of water to the boil and in it dissolve the sugar. Cool to blood heat, then add to the marrows together with the yeast and nutrient and the juice of the lemons.

2. Cover and keep in a warm place to ferment for 5 days, stirring twice daily. Strain the liquid carefully off the pulp and transfer to a fermenting jar.

3. Fit an air-lock and leave to ferment on, racking when the wine starts to clear.

4. When the fermentation has ended and the wine cleared, bottle and store in a cool dark place to mature for at least 6 months.

PARSNIP

This is one of the most popular country wines, very like a light sherry. You should certainly use old, withered parsnips as these have more sugar. Take care not to overcook them, or the wine will be difficult to clear. This recipe can also be used to make turnip wine.

	IMP	US	METRIC
old parsnips	4 lbs	3¼ lbs	1.8 kg
sugar	3 lbs	2½ lbs	1.4 kg
raisins	8 ozs	7 ozs	226 g
lemons	2	2	2
Camden tablet	1	1	1
pectin enzyme	1 tsp	1 tsp	1 tsp
grape tannin	½ tsp	½ tsp	½ tsp
water	1 gallon	1 gallon	4.5 l
wine yeast			
yeast nutrient			

1. Scrub the parsnips, peel them and slice coarsely into 1 gallon (4.5 l) of cold water. Stir in the crushed Camden tablet and pectin enzyme, and leave to steep for 24 hours.
2. Bring to the boil and simmer very gently in an open vessel until the parsnips are just tender.
3. Strain the liquid off, taking care not to wring or press the pulp too much. Dissolve the sugar in the liquid, leave until comfortably warm, then add the yeast and nutrient, the chopped raisins, grape tannin and juice of the lemons.
4. Keep well covered in a warm place to ferment for 7 days, stirring twice daily.
5. Strain into a fermenting jar, close off with bung and air-lock and leave to ferment on, racking when the wine begins to clear.
6. When all fermentation has ceased and the wine is brilliantly clear, bottle and store in a cool dark place to mature for at least 6 months.

PUMPKIN

Wine from pumpkin can be made with Demerara sugar to give a rich golden colour. This recipe can also be used to make wines from marrows and melons.

	IMP	US	METRIC
ripe pumpkin	5 lbs	4½ lbs	2.3 kg
sugar	3 lbs	2½ lbs	1.4 kg
lemons	2	2	2
root ginger	1 oz	$7/8$ oz	28 g
Camden tablet	1	1	1
pectin enzyme	1 tsp	1 tsp	1 tsp
water	1 gallon	1 gallon	4.5 l
wine yeast			
yeast nutrient			

1. Wash the pumpkin, peel and remove the seeds and slice into a vessel, add the bruised ginger and cover with 6 pints (3.4 l) of cold water. Stir in the crushed Camden tablet and pectin enzyme and leave for 24 hours. Bring a further 2 pints (1.1 l) of water to the boil and in it dissolve the sugar. Cool to blood heat, then add to the marrows together with the yeast and nutrient and the juice of the lemons.

2. Cover and keep in a warm place to ferment for 5 days, stirring twice daily. Strain the liquid carefully off the pulp and transfer to a fermenting jar.

3. Fit an air-lock and leave to ferment on, racking when the wine starts to clear.

4. When the fermentation has ended and the wine cleared, bottle and store in a cool dark place to mature for at least 6 months.

PEA POD (OR PEA SHUCK)

A wine for free, almost. Once the peas have been removed, the empty pods can be used to make one of the traditional old country wines.

	IMP	US	METRIC
pea pods, or shucks	4 lbs	3¼ lbs	1.8 kg
sugar	3 lbs	2½ lbs	1.4 kg
lemons	2	2	2
Camden tablet	1	1	1
pectin enzyme	1 tsp	1 tsp	1 tsp
grape tannin	½ tsp	½ tsp	½ tsp
water	1 gallon	1 gallon	4.5 l
wine yeast			
yeast nutrient			

1. Wash the pods and check that no peas are left in them. Cover with 1 gallon (4.5 l) of boiling water and when this has cooled, add the crushed Camden tablet and pectin enzyme. Cover and leave for 24 hours.

2. Bring to the boil, cover and simmer gently until the pods are tender. Strain the liquid and pour over the sugar, stirring well to dissolve it. When the liquid is just comfortably warm, add the yeast and nutrient, the grape tannin and juice of the lemons.

3. Cover and leave to ferment in a warm place for 4–5 days, stirring twice daily.

4. Transfer to a fermenting jar, close off with bung and air-lock and leave to ferment on, racking when the wine begins to clear.

5. When all fermentation has ended and the wine is clear, bottle and store in a cool dark place to mature for at least 6 months.

POTATO

This is one of the most potent of the home-made wines and should be made with care. On no account should green potatoes be used: they contain a lethal poison. Use only old potatoes, preferably ones beginning to wrinkle, and cut away any green parts. White sugar can be used with this recipe, but Demerara sugar gives the wine a better colour.

	IMP	US	METRIC
old potatoes	2 lbs	1¾ lbs	905 g
sugar	2 lbs	1¾ lbs	905 g
raisins	1 lb	14 ozs	453 g
pearl barley	1 lb	14 ozs	453 g
oranges	3	3	3
water	1 gallon	1 gallon	4.5 l
wine yeast			
yeast nutrient			

1. Scrub the potatoes well, without peeling, chop coarsely and put into a boiling vessel with the pearl barley.
2. Cover with 1 gallon (4.5 l) of water, bring to the boil and simmer gently until the potatoes are just tender, but not mushy. Remove any scum that rises to the surface.
3. Strain the liquid over the sugar and dissolve thoroughly.
4. When the liquid is comfortably warm, add the yeast and nutrient, the minced raisins and juice of the oranges.
5. Cover well and keep in a warm place to ferment for 7 days, stirring twice daily.
6. Strain into a fermenting jar, close off with bung and air-lock and leave to ferment on, racking when the wine starts to clear.
7. When fermentation has ceased entirely and the wine is clear, bottle and store in a cool dark place to mature for at least 1 year.

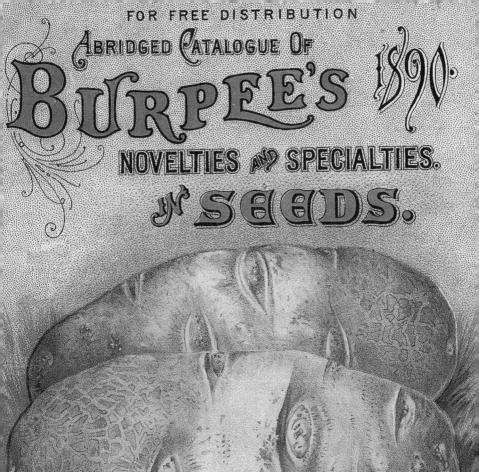

FOR FREE DISTRIBUTION

ABRIDGED CATALOGUE OF

BURPEE'S 1890.

NOVELTIES AND SPECIALTIES.

IN SEEDS.

BURPEE'S EXTRA EARLY POTATO.

STECHER LITH CO. ROCHESTER N.Y.

W. ATLEE BURPEE & CO.
WAB

SEED GROWERS.

RUNNER BEAN

Runner beans – also called green beans or string beans – make one of the true old country wines. Prepare them as you would for cooking, but if they are old (the best kind to use), break them by hand instead of slicing with a knife, or too much starch will be released and haze the wine.

	IMP	US	METRIC
runner beans	2 lbs	1¾ lbs	905 g
sugar	2 lbs	1¾ lbs	905 g
sultanas	1 lb	14 ozs	453 g
grapefruits	2	2	2
Camden tablet	1	1	1
pectin enzyme	1 tsp	1 tsp	1 tsp
grape tannin	½ tsp	½ tsp	½ tsp
water	1 gallon	1 gallon	4.5 l
wine yeast			
yeast nutrient			

1. Slice or break the beans into 1 gallon (4.5 l) of cold water, stir in the crushed Camden tablet and pectin enzyme, and leave covered for 24 hours. Bring to the boil and simmer gently until just tender.
2. Strain the liquid, discarding the beans, and pour over the sugar, stirring until dissolved.
3. When the liquid is comfortably warm, add the yeast and nutrient, the chopped sultanas, grape tannin and juice of the grapefruits.
4. Leave well covered in a warm place to ferment for 4 days, stirring twice daily.
5. Strain the liquid into a fermenting jar, close off with an air-lock and leave to ferment on, racking when the wine begins to clear.
6. When all fermentation has ceased and the wine completely cleared, bottle and store in a cool dark place to mature for at least 6 months.

TOMATO

A surprisingly pleasant rosé wine can be made from tomatoes – any variety – so this is an excellent way to use up any surplus ripe or over-ripe fruit.

	IMP	US	METRIC
tomatoes	6 lbs	5¼ lbs	2.7 kg
sugar	3 lbs	2½ lbs	1.4 kg
lemon	1	1	1
root ginger	1 oz	⁷/₈ oz	28 g
Camden tablet	1	1	1
pectin enzyme	1 tsp	1 tsp	1 tsp
water	7 pints	7 pints	4 l
wine yeast			
yeast nutrient			

1. Chop or crush the tomatoes (no need to skin them), bruise the root ginger and cover both with 5 pints (2.8 l) of cold water. Add the crushed Camden tablet and pectin enzyme and leave to steep for 24 hours.
2. Bring a further 2 pints (1.1 l) of water to the boil and dissolve the sugar in it. Allow this syrup to cool to blood heat, then add to the tomato pulp, followed by the yeast and nutrient and the juice of the lemon.
3. Cover and leave to ferment in a warm place for 4 days, stirring twice daily.
4. Strain the liquid off the pulp, pressing well to extract the juice. Measure and if necessary add cool boiled water to make up to 1 gallon (4.5 l). Transfer to a fermenting jar, fit bung and air-lock and leave to ferment on, racking when the wine begins clearing.
5. When fermentation has ceased entirely and the wine is clear, bottle and store in a cool dark place to mature for at least 9 months, preferably a year.

MEAD,
BEERS
AND OTHER
DRINKS

MEAD

Mead, or fermented honey, is one of the oldest alcoholic pale honey
from apple, clover or lime blossom makes a light, delicate wine; darker
honey, such as heather, has a stronger flavour and is best made as a
sweet wine. Avoid using imported or blended honey as this is often
difficult to clear; and for best results, use a mead yeast.

Dry	IMP	US	METRIC
light honey	3½ lbs	3 lbs	1.6 kg
lemons	2	2	2
grape tannin	1 tsp	1 tsp	1 tsp
water	1 gallon	1 gallon	4.5 l
mead yeast			
yeast nutrient			
Sweet			
medium or dark honey	4½ lbs	4 lbs	2 kg
lemons	2	2	2
grape tannin	1 tsp	1 tsp	1 tsp
water	1 gallon	1 gallon	4.5 l
mead yeast			
yeast nutrient			

1. Heat the honey gently in 1 gallon (4.5 l) of water until dissolved,
   removing any scum that rises to the surface.
2. Leave until comfortably warm, then add the yeast and nutrient, the
   grape tannin and juice of the lemons.
3. Cover well and leave to ferment in a warm place for 3 days, stirring
   twice daily.
4. Strain into a fermenting jar, close off with an air-lock and leave to
   ferment on, racking when the wine starts to clear.
5. When all fermentation has ceased and the wine is completely clear,
   bottle and store in a cool dark place to mature for at least a year,
   preferably 18 months.

HOP BEER

The bitter-tasting hop has been used to flavour beer for some 500 years. The beer is made by fermenting malt (roasted barley) with a brewing yeast; though most amateur beer- makers nowadays prefer to simplify the process by using malt extract in place of pure malt. Beer should only be stored in beer or cider bottles.

	IMP	US	METRIC
malt extract	1 lb	14 ozs	453 g
sugar	1 lb	14 ozs	453 g
dried hops	1 oz	$^7/_8$ oz	28 g
salt	½ tsp	½ tsp	½ tsp
water	1 gallon	1 gallon	4.5 l
brewing yeast			

1. Heat the water and stir in the hops, keeping a few back to add later. Bring to the boil, cover the vessel and continue boiling for 30 minutes, adding the remaining hops at the end to boost flavour.
2. Strain the liquid into a strong polythene vessel and add the malt extract, sugar and salt, stirring well until all is dissolved.
3. Leave the liquid until just comfortably warm, then add the brewing yeast. Cover well and leave in a warm place to ferment for about 5 days, using a plastic skimmer each day to take off any froth that appears on the surface. When the ring of froth at the centre has shrunk to about 2 inches (51 mm) in diameter, rack the beer into a clean vessel and stir in an extra 2 ozs (1¾ ozs US; 56 g) of sugar.
4. When the sugar is thoroughly dissolved, siphon the beer into sterilised beer or cider bottles and seal with crown corks or ordinary corks (*not* screw caps). Tie the corks down firmly.
5. Store the bottles in a warm place for 2 days, to encourage the ferment, then move them into a cooler temperature to allow the beer to clear. It can be drunk after 2 weeks, but improves if kept a little longer.

HOPS

DANDELION BEER

Long before hops became the main flavouring ingredient of beer, country ale-wives used the milder-flavoured dandelion, nettle, and other herbs. Some of these traditional cottage beers can still be made, and are especially refreshing as a brewing yeast summer drink.

	IMP	US	METRIC
dandelion roots and leaves	8 ozs	7 ozs	226 g
sugar	1 lb	14 ozs	453 g
lemons	2	2	2
root ginger	1 oz	$^7/_8$ oz	28 g
tartaric acid	¼ oz	¼ oz	7 g
water	1 gallon	1 gallon	4.5 l

1. To 1 gallon (4.5 l) of water add the bruised dandelion roots and leaves and the bruised root ginger, cover and boil together for 10 minutes.
2. Strain the liquid into a strong polythene vessel and add the sugar and juice of the lemons, stirring well till dissolved.
3. When the liquid is just comfortably warm, add the brewing yeast and tartaric acid.
4. Cover closely and leave to ferment in a warm place for 3 days, using a plastic skimmer to take off any froth that rises to the surface.
5. Strain the beer into sterilised beer or cider bottles and seal off with corks (*not* screw caps). Tie the corks down firmly.
6. Store the bottles upright in a cool place for a week before drinking.

GINGER BEER

Long before hops became the main flavouring ingredient of beer, country ale-wives used the milder-flavoured dandelion, nettle, and other herbs. Some of these traditional cottage beers can still be made, and are especially refreshing as a brewing yeast summer drink.

	IMP	US	METRIC
root ginger	1½ ozs	1¼ ozs	42 g
sugar	2 lbs	1¾ lbs	905 g
lemons	2	2	2
tartaric acid	¼ oz	¼ oz	7 g
water	1 gallon	1 gallon	4.5 l
brewing yeast			

1. Pare the rind thinly from the lemons, taking care to avoid the white pith. Squeeze the lemons and put the juice and rind together in a polythene vessel.
2. Add the sugar and the well-bruised ginger, and cover with 1 gallon (4.5 l) of boiling water.
3. Stir well, and when the liquid is just comfortably warm, add the yeast and the tartaric acid.
5. Cover and leave to ferment in a warm place for 24 hours.
6. Strain into sterilised beer or cider bottles and seal off with corks (not screw caps).

Ginger beer can be drunk immediately.

HONEY BEER

Long before hops became the main flavouring ingredient of beer, country ale-wives used the milder-flavoured dandelion, nettle, and other herbs. Some of these traditional cottage beers can still be made, and are especially refreshing as a brewing yeast summer drink.

	IMP	US	METRIC
clear honey	4 ozs	3½ ozs	113 g
sugar	1 lb	14 ozs	453 g
lemons	3	3	3
ground ginger	1 oz	$^7/_8$ oz	28 g
fresh lime juice	2 fl. ozs	2 fl. ozs	57 ml
water	1 gallon	1 gallon	4.5 l
brewing yeast			

1. Dissolve the ginger in 4 pints (2.25 l) of boiling water, cover and simmer for 30 minutes.
2. Pour the liquid into a strong polythene vessel and add the honey and sugar, stirring well until dissolved. Stir in an additional 4 pints (2.25 l) of cold water, together with the lime juice and the juice of the lemons. Test that the liquid is just comfortably warm before adding the yeast, then cover the vessel and leave in a warm place to ferment for 24 hours. Strain into a clean vessel, allow an hour or so for the beer to settle, then bottle it, using beer or cider bottles only. Seal off with corks (*not* screw caps) and tie the corks down firmly.
3. Store upright in a cool place for a week before drinking.

NETTLE BEER

Long before hops became the main flavouring ingredient of beer, country ale-wives used the milder-flavoured dandelion, nettle, and other herbs. Some of these traditional cottage beers can still be made, and are especially refreshing as a brewing yeast summer drink.

	IMP	US	METRIC
young nettles	1 gallon	1 gallon	4.5 l
sugar	12 ozs	10½ ozs	339 g
lemon	1	1	1
malt	2 lbs	1¾ lbs	905 g
sarsaparilla	2 ozs	1¾ ozs	56 g
root ginger	¼ oz	¼ oz	7 g
dried hops	1 oz	$^{7}/_{8}$ oz	28 g
water	1 gallon	1 gallon	4.5 l
brewing yeast			

1. To 1 gallon (4.5 l) of water add the washed nettles, the bruised ginger, malt, hops and sarsaparilla, cover and boil together for 15 minutes. Strain the liquid into a polythene vessel and add the sugar and juice of the lemon, stirring well to dissolve.
2. When the liquid is just comfortably cool, add the yeast.
3. Cover and keep in a warm place to ferment for 3 days, using a plastic skimmer to take off any froth that rises to the surface.
4. Strain the beer into sterilised beer or cider bottles, seal off with corks (*not* screw caps) and tie the corks down firmly.
5. Store the bottles upright in a cool place for a week before drinking.

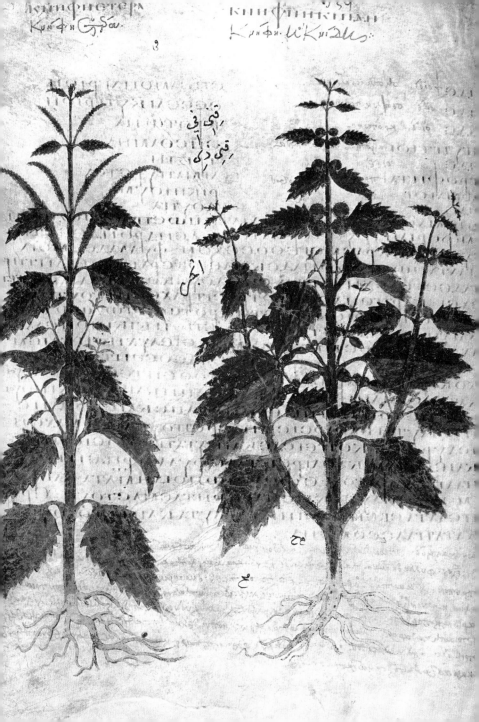

قنى فى
قنى دى

اجح

ﺲ

ﻊ

SPRUCE BEER

Long before hops became the main flavouring ingredient of beer, country ale-wives used the milder-flavoured dandelion, nettle, and other herbs. Some of these traditional cottage beers can still be made, and are especially refreshing as a brewing yeast summer drink.

	IMP	US	METRIC
spruce fir twigs	4 ozs	3½ ozs	113 g
or spruce essence	1 tbsp	1 tbsp	1 tbsp
sugar	1 lb	14 ozs	453 g
dried hops	1 oz	7/8 oz	28 g
root ginger	½ oz	½ oz	14 g
water	1 gallon	1 gallon	4.5 l
brewing yeast			

1. If using spruce twigs (outer twigs only), add them to 1 gallon (4.5 l) of water together with the bruised ginger and hops, and boil together for 15 minutes. If using spruce essence, boil the ginger and hops alone.
2. Strain the liquid into a polythene vessel and stir in the sugar (and spruce essence, if using).
3. When the liquid is just comfortably cool, add the brewing yeast.
4. Cover well and leave in a warm place to ferment for 2 days, using a plastic skimmer to take off any froth that rises to the surface.
5. Strain into sterilised beer or cider bottles and seal off with corks (*not* screw caps). Tie the corks down firmly.
6. Store the bottles upright in a cool place for a week before drinking.

IDAHO.

THE STORRS HARRISON CO.

CHAMPION.

ECLIPSE.

1895

SANGRIA

Black currant, elderberry, damson, plum... any of the home-made red wines can be used to make this delicious drink, perfect for a warm summer's evening. The name itself comes from the Spanish *sangaree*: 'a refreshing drink made with wine'.

2 bottles of red wine
1 bottle of lemonade
1 small wineglass of brandy
fruit in season

1. Wash the fruit – a selection of oranges, strawberries, apples, peaches, or whatever is fresh – and slice into a large jug.
2. Pour in the wine, lemonade and brandy, and stir in a generous cupful of cracked ice.
3. When the sangria is thoroughly chilled, serve it in large wineglasses with the sliced fruit.

PUNCH

Hot punch is surely the most civilised way to banish the cold of a winter's night, or to welcome friends to the warmth of the fireside. It's traditionally made with a good red wine – any of the dark red home-made wines can be used – or, as a variation, it can include a white wine such as apple, rhubarb or elderflower.

½ bottle of wine
½ bottle of Jamaica rum
3 lemons, 1 large orange
sugar 8 ozs (7 ozs US; 226 g)
¼ teaspoon each of ground cinnamon and
ground clove

1. Grate or pare the rind very thinly from the lemons, taking care to avoid any white pith. Put the rind into a boiling vessel together with the cinnamon, clove and sugar, and add the rum and the juice of the lemons. Cover with 2 pints (1.1 l) of water and heat very gently, without boiling, to dissolve the sugar.
2. Strain immediately into a warmed punch bowl or other suitable container, and stir in the wine.
3. Decorate with a little grated nutmeg and thinly-cut slices of orange.

APPLEADE

These are sweetened drinks made from fresh fruit juice and water, simple and wholesome, and so much nicer than any commercially made product. If you prefer fizzy ades, reduce the water to 1½ pints (852 ml) and add a ½ pint (284 ml) of soda water after straining off the fruit.

	IMP	US	METRIC
sweet, juicy apples	2 lbs	1¾ lbs	905 g
lemon	1	1	1
water	2 pints	2 pints	1.1 l
sugar to taste			

1. Chop the apples, including core and peel, taking care not to lose any juice.
2. Grate or peel the lemon rind (avoiding the white pith) and put into a heat-resistant jug with the apple pieces.
3. Cover with the boiling water, then add the juice of the lemon and sweeten to individual taste.
4. Leave until cold, then strain and serve in glasses with cracked ice and a few sprigs of fresh mint to decorate.

CHERRYADE

These are sweetened drinks made from fresh fruit juice and water, simple and wholesome, and so much nicer than any commercially made product. If you prefer fizzy ades, reduce the water to 1½ pints (852 ml) and add a ½ pint (284 ml) of soda water after straining off the fruit.

	IMP	US	METRIC
ripe cherries	1 lb	14 ozs	453 g
lemon	1	1	1
water	2 pints	2 pints	1.1 l
sugar to taste			

1. Halve the cherries, discarding the stones.
2. Grate or peel the lemon rind (avoiding the white pith) and put into a heat-resistant jug together with the cherries.
3. Cover with the boiling water, add the juice of the lemon and sweeten to individual taste.
4. Leave until cold, then strain and serve in glasses with cracked ice and a cherry sprig to decorate.

ROYAL

LES DISTILLATEURS AU MOINS TOUJOURS SES FILS

CITRON

LE MEILLEU

DE TOUS LES SIROPS

E. PICHOT   DÉPOSÉ

LEMONADE

These are sweetened drinks made from fresh fruit juice and water, simple and wholesome, and so much nicer than any commercially made product. If you prefer fizzy ades, reduce the water to 1½ pints (852 ml) and add a ½ pint (284 ml) of soda water after straining off the fruit.

	IMP	US	METRIC
large lemons	3	3	3
water	2 pints	2 pints	1.1 l
sugar to taste			

1. Wash the lemons and slice up into thin rings, taking care not to lose any juice.
2. Put the slices into a heat-resistant jug, cover with the boiling water and sweeten to individual taste.
3. Leave for 30 minutes, then strain.
4. When cold, serve in glasses with cracked ice and decorate with lemon slices and a few sprigs of lemon balm.

ORANGEADE

These are sweetened drinks made from fresh fruit juice and water, simple and wholesome, and so much nicer than any commercially made product. If you prefer fizzy ades, reduce the water to 1½ pints (852 ml) and add a ½ pint (284 ml) of soda water after straining off the fruit.

	IMP	US	METRIC
large juicy oranges	4	4	4
water	2 pints	2 pints	1.1 l
sugar to sweeten			

1. Grate or pare the orange rinds thinly, taking care not to include any white pith.
2. Put the rind into a heat-resistant jug and cover with the boiling water, then add the juice of the oranges and sweeten to individual taste.
3. Leave until cold, then strain. Serve with cracked ice and slices of orange to decorate.

RASPBERRYADE

These are sweetened drinks made from fresh fruit juice and water, simple and wholesome, and so much nicer than any commercially made product. If you prefer fizzy ades, reduce the water to 1½ pints (852 ml) and add a ½ pint (284 ml) of soda water after straining off the fruit.

	IMP	US	METRIC
ripe raspberries	1 lb	14 ozs	453 g
lemons	2	2	2
water	2 pints	2 pints	1.1 l
sugar to sweeten			

1. Slice the lemons into thin rings and put into a heat-resistant jug together with the raspberries.
2. Cover with the boiling water and sweeten to individual taste. Leave for 30 minutes, then strain.
3. When cold, serve with cracked ice, adding raspberries and lemon rings to decorate.

FRUIT SYRUPS

These are made to a simple recipe and are an excellent base for a variety of drinks. They can be served diluted with iced water or soda, stirred into milk for milk shakes, dissolved in hot water for winter warmth and goodness, poured over ice-creams and puddings, or added to jellies, blancmanges and custards for extra flavour. Syrups can be made from any of the berry or currant fruits, as well as damsons, oranges, rosehips, and so on. You'll need 1 lb of ripe fruit 8 ozs of sugar (453 g: 226 g), and a preserving or bottling jar, sterilised along with its screw and cap by immersion in boiling water for 20 minutes.

Add water as follows:	IMP, US	METRIC
apricot	½ pint	284 ml
blackberry	¼ pint	142 ml
black currant	¼ pint	142 ml
blueberry	¼ pint	142 ml
damson	½ pint	284 ml
elderberry	¼ pint	142 ml
loganberry	¼ pint	142 ml
orange	½ pint	284 ml
plum	½ pint	284 ml
raspberry	none	none
red currant	¼ pint	142 ml
rosehip	1 pint	568 ml
strawberry	none	none

1. To extract 1 pint (568 ml) of fruit juice, put the washed fruit into a heavy-based saucepan and crush it, or chop it finely, depending on its type. Remove the stones from fruit such as apricots and plums; and for citrus fruits, use the juice and grated peel only.
2. Heat the water gently, stirring the fruit to prevent it sticking. Cook for 1 hour (except rosehips – 15 minutes only), pressing the fruit well from time to time to extract the juice.
3. Strain the liquid off, using a jelly bag or several thicknesses of nylon or muslin. Measure the liquid, and if necessary make up to 1 pint (568 ml) with freshly boiled water.
4. Stir in 8 ozs (226 g) of sugar and heat gently until the sugar has completely dissolved – do *not* allow the syrup to boil.
5. Pour the syrup into the warmed bottling or preserving jar, filling it to within no more than ½ inch (13 mm) of the top, and leave to cool. Screw on the cap, then loosen it slightly with a reverse half-turn.
6. Put the jar into a saucepan of cold water, standing it on a rack or a folded cloth to keep it off the saucepan base.
7. Bring the water very slowly to the boil- over a period of an hour, if possible – then let it simmer for 30 minutes.
8. Lift the jar carefully out and stand it on a wooden surface or a folded cloth – if the surface is too cold the jar may crack.
9. Screw the cap down tightly, and leave the jar to cool.
10. Store the syrup in a dark place to preserve its colour and flavour. It will keep for a long period, but should be used up quickly once the jar is opened.

GER

$ 3.00 EACH

9

VEGETABLE SEEDS
                                    PKT
1 EXPRESS CUCUMBER ...10 ¢
2 ROCKY FORD MELON   10 ¢
3 FORDHOOK FANCY TOMATO .10 ¢
4 YELLOW SIBLEY SQUASH   10 ¢
5 BLUE GEM WATER MELON ... 5 ¢

5 PACKETS for 25 CTS.

5

4

1

8 HARVEST MOON COREOPSIS...1

9 MANDA'S TRIUMPH ROSE.....2

10 MINIATURE TRADESCANTIA 1

11 WHITE PHENOMENAL FUCHSIA 1

THE 6 PLANTS FOR 50 CTS

8

10

7

6

FISH COLLECTION $1.35

1 GLASS GLOBE

2 GOLD FISHES

1 PEARL FISH

2

1 SILVER FISH

SHELLS, LIVE MOS

& FISH

REID'S Annual Catalogue 1896

THE TIMBRELL STRAWBERRY

THE ELDORADO BLACKBERRY

BLACKBERRY CORDIAL

The name cordial comes from the Latin *cordialis*: 'of the heart', and was given by country wives to special potions which they believed had the power to invigorate the heart and restore the spirits. An English medical book of 1541 refers to 'al thinges whiche be cordiall, that is to say, which do in any wise comfort the hart'. Nowadays, cordials are more often taken to relieve sore throats and other cold symptoms.

	IMP	US	METRIC
ripe blackberries	1 lb	14 ozs	453 g
sugar	1 lb	14 ozs	453 g
clear honey	8 ozs	7 ozs	226 g
white wine	1 pint	1 pint	568 ml
vinegar			

1. Wash the blackberries thoroughly, put into a large earthenware or polythene bowl and crush.
2. Cover with the wine vinegar and leave for a week, pressing the fruit twice daily with a wooden spoon to extract the juice.
3. Strain the liquid into a saucepan (discard the fruit pulp for cooking purposes) and add the honey and sugar.
4. Bring slowly to the boil and simmer gently for 5 minutes, stirring continuously.
5. Leave the cordial to cool, then pour it into a bottle and close off with a cork or screw cap. Store in a cool dark place.
6. To take, dissolve 1 tablespoon of the cordial in a tumbler of hot water.

LANCASHIRE LAD GOOSEBERRY

NORTH STAR CURRANT

WILDER EARLY PEAR

AMERICAN BLUSH APPLE

CURRANT CORDIAL

The name cordial comes from the Latin *cordialis*: 'of the heart', and was given by country wives to special potions which they believed had the power to invigorate the heart and restore the spirits. An English medical book of 1541 refers to 'al thinges whiche be cordiall, that is to say, which do in any wise comfort the hart'. Nowadays, cordials are more often taken to relieve sore throats and other cold symptoms.

	IMP	US	METRIC
red currants	1 lb	14 ozs	453 g
raspberries	8 ozs	7 ozs	226 g
sugar	1 lb	14 ozs	453 g
water	2½ pints	2½ pints	1.4 l

1. Wash and stalk the fruit and put into a saucepan. Crush well, then add 8 ozs of the sugar (7 ozs US; 226 g) and 1 pint of water (568 ml).
2. Bring slowly to the boil and simmer gently for 5 minutes, stirring continuously.
3. Strain the liquid into a heat-resistant jug (discard the fruit pulp for cooking purposes) and leave to one side.
4. Bring the remaining 1½ pints of water (852 ml) to the boil and in it dissolve the rest of the sugar. Add this syrup to the jug and stir in thoroughly. Currant cordial can be taken undiluted.

DAMSON CORDIAL

The name cordial comes from the Latin *cordialis*: 'of the heart', and was given by country wives to special potions which they believed had the power to invigorate the heart and restore the spirits. An English medical book of 1541 refers to 'al thinges whiche be cordiall, that is to say, which do in any wise comfort the hart'. Nowadays, cordials are more often taken to relieve sore throats and other cold symptoms.

	IMP	US	METRIC
ripe damsons	1 lb	14 ozs	453 g
elderberries	8 ozs	7 ozs	226 g
sugar	3 lbs	2½ lbs	1.4 kg
clear honey	4 tbsps	4 tbsps	4 tbsps
water	2 pints	2 pints	1.1 l

1. Stone the damsons and put into a container. Bruise them well, pour over the boiling water, add half a dozen cracked damson stones and leave to soak for 24 hours.
2. Meanwhile, strip the elderberries from their stalks, put them into a separate container and crush them.
3. Bring the damsons and the water in which they have soaked to the boil and simmer gently for 15 minutes. Strain the liquid over the elderberries (discard the damson pulp for cooking purposes), and leave to soak for a further 24 hours.
4. Bring the elderberries and the juice in which they have soaked to the boil, stir in the sugar and honey and simmer gently for 15 minutes.
5. When cool, strain the cordial carefully into bottles and close off with corks or screw caps. Store in a cool dark place.
6. To take, dissolve 1 tablespoon of the cordial in a tumbler of hot water.

RHUBARB CORDIAL

The name cordial comes from the Latin *cordialis*: 'of the heart', and was given by country wives to special potions which they believed had the power to invigorate the heart and restore the spirits. An English medical book of 1541 refers to 'al thinges whiche be cordiall, that is to say, which do in any wise comfort the hart'. Nowadays, cordials are more often taken to relieve sore throats and other cold symptoms.

	IMP	US	METRIC
red rhubarb	2 lbs	1¾ lbs	905 g
root ginger	¼ oz	¼ oz	7 g
sugar	4 ozs	3½ ozs	113 g
cloves	2	2	2
water	2 pints	2 pints	1.1 l

1. Chop the rhubarb coarsely and put into a saucepan together with the sugar, cloves and bruised ginger.
2. Cover with the water, bring slowly to the boil and simmer until the rhubarb is tender.
3. Strain off the liquid (discard the fruit pulp for cooking purposes) and leave until cool.
4. Rhubarb cordial can be taken undiluted.

BARLEY WATER

Barley water has long been regarded as a restorative, used in folk medicine to treat throat troubles, asthma and kidney ailments. It's also a very nourishing drink.

	IMP	US	METRIC
pearl barley	4 ozs	3½ ozs	113 g
sugar	2 ozs	1¾ ozs	56 g
lemon rind			
water			

1. Put the washed barley into a saucepan and add sufficient water just to cover. Blanch the barley by boiling it for 3 minutes, then strain it well. Throw the water away.
2. Pare half a lemon rind thinly, taking care to avoid the white pith. Put the rind into a heat-resistant jug, together with the barley and the sugar. Pour over 2 pints (1.1 l) of boiling water, stir well to dissolve the sugar, and leave to cool.
3. Strain the barley water before drinking it.

LEMON BARLEY WATER

Barley water has long been regarded as a restorative, used in folk medicine to treat throat troubles, asthma and kidney ailments. It's also a very nourishing drink, and can be flavoured with the fresh juice of lemon for added vitamin content.

	IMP	US	METRIC
pearl barley	4 ozs	3½ ozs	113 g
sugar	2 ozs	1¾ ozs	56 g
lemon juice	2 lemons		
lemon rind			
water			

1. Put the washed barley into a saucepan and add sufficient water just to cover. Blanch the barley by boiling it for 3 minutes, then strain it well. Throw the water away.
2. Pare half a lemon rind thinly, taking care to avoid the white pith. Put the rind into a heat-resistant jug, together with the barley and the sugar. Pour over 2 pints (1.1 l) of boiling water, stir well to dissolve the sugar, and leave to cool.
3. When cooled, add the lemon juice.
4. Strain the lemon barley water before drinking it.

ORANGE BARLEY WATER

Barley water has long been regarded as a restorative, used in folk medicine to treat throat troubles, asthma and kidney ailments. It's also a very nourishing drink, and can be flavoured with the fresh juice of orange for added vitamin content.

	IMP	US	METRIC
pearl barley	4 ozs	3½ ozs	113 g
sugar	2 ozs	1¾ ozs	56 g
orange juice	2 large oranges		
orange rind			
water			

1. Put the washed barley into a saucepan and add sufficient water just to cover. Blanch the barley by boiling it for 3 minutes, then strain it well. Throw the water away.
2. Pare half an orange rind thinly, taking care to avoid the white pith. Put the rind into a heat-resistant jug, together with the barley and the sugar. Pour over 2 pints (1.1 l) of boiling water, stir well to dissolve the sugar, and leave to cool.
3. When cooled, add the orange juice.
4. Strain the orange barley water before drinking it.

FRUIT AND VEGETABLE JUICES

No drink is easier or quicker to make than fresh citrus juice, which comes neatly packaged in an orange, lemon, lime or grapefruit skin and merely needs squeezing into a glass. Other juices weren't intended by Nature to be quite so easy to extract; but with the help of an electric liquidiser they take only a few minutes to prepare, and are so much more satisfying than chemical-based products.

These fruit and vegetable drinks can be made either with soda water or plain water. Because fresh juice does not keep well, the recipes given here are sufficient for one glass only. However, if you want to prepare it in larger quantities, one standard bottle of juice can be obtained by trebling the amount of ingredients in each recipe and increasing the amount of water to make up the bulk. To preserve the juice, add one powdered Camden tablet per bottle, and sterilise the bottles before use by soaking in a Camden solution or by immersing in boiling water. Use screw-top glass bottles if you intend using the juice within a few days and store in a cool place, preferably a refrigerator. If you want to keep the juice longer, use screw-top plastic bottles and store in the icebox.

NEW AND Choicest VEGETABLE Specialties

These 9 SPECIALTIES for 30 Cts., Postpaid.

1. TOMATO—Alneer's New Beauty.
2. RADISH—Alneer's New Fourteen Day.
3. BEET—Alneer's New Columbia.
4. CABBAGE—Excelsior, Large, Late Flat Dutch
5. CORN, SWEET—Alneer's Extra Early
   Columbia.
6. ONION—Alneer's Selected Yellow
   Globe Danvers.
7. MUSKMELON—Grand Rapids.
8. WATERMELON—McIver's Wonderful
   Sugar.
9. LETTUCE—California All Heart.

APPLE JUICE

These fruit and vegetable drinks can be made either with soda water or plain water, and the icing sugar here is optional. Because fresh juice does not keep well, the recipes given here are sufficient for one glass only. However, if you want to prepare it in larger quantities, one standard bottle of juice can be obtained by trebling the amount of ingredients in each recipe and increasing the amount of water to make up the bulk. To preserve the juice, add one powdered Camden tablet per bottle, and sterilise the bottles before use by soaking in a Camden solution or by immersing in boiling water. Use screw-top glass bottles if you intend using the juice within a few days and store in a cool place, preferably a refrigerator. If you want to keep the juice longer, use screw-top plastic bottles and store in the icebox.

large eating apples	2 large
water	7 fl.ozs (213 ml)
icing sugar	3 teaspoons

1. Chop up the apples, discarding the cores.
2. Put the apples in the liquidiser along with the water and icing sugar.
3. Liquidise, pour into a glass and serve immediately.

BERRY JUICE

These fruit and vegetable drinks can be made either with soda water or plain water, and the icing sugar here is optional. Because fresh juice does not keep well, the recipes given here are sufficient for one glass only. However, if you want to prepare it in larger quantities, one standard bottle of juice can be obtained by trebling the amount of ingredients in each recipe and increasing the amount of water to make up the bulk. To preserve the juice, add one powdered Camden tablet per bottle, and sterilise the bottles before use by soaking in a Camden solution or by immersing in boiling water. Use screw-top glass bottles if you intend using the juice within a few days and store in a cool place, preferably a refrigerator. If you want to keep the juice longer, use screw-top plastic bottles and store in the icebox. Any kind of berry can be used for this delicious juice.

ripe berries	6 ozs (170 g)
water	5 fl.ozs (142 ml)
icing sugar	3 teaspoons

1. Put the ripe berries in the liquidiser along with the water and icing sugar.
2. Liquidise, pour into a glass and serve immediately.

SPRING 1896

don
Raspberry

CATALOGUE OF
GREEN'S
NURSERY Co.

COPYRIGHTED 1895
BY C.A. GREEN.
ROCHESTER, N.Y.

CARROT JUICE

These fruit and vegetable drinks can be made either with soda water
or plain water, and the icing sugar here is optional. Because fresh
juice does not keep well, the recipes given here are sufficient for one
glass only. However, if you want to prepare it in larger quantities, one
standard bottle of juice can be obtained by trebling the amount of
ingredients in each recipe and increasing the amount of water to make
up the bulk. To preserve the juice, add one powdered Camden tablet
per bottle, and sterilise the bottles before use by soaking in a Camden
solution or by immersing in boiling water. Use screw-top glass bottles
if you intend using the juice within a few days and store in a cool place,
preferably a refrigerator. If you want to keep the juice longer, use
screw-top plastic bottles and store in the icebox.

carrots	2 medium
water	7 fl.ozs (213ml)
icing sugar	2 teaspoons
fresh lemon juice	1 teaspoon

1. Scrape and chop the carrots.
2. Put the carrots in the liquidiser along with the water, icing sugar
   and lemon juice.
3. Liquidise, pour into a glass and serve immediately.

CUCUMBER JUICE

These fruit and vegetable drinks can be made either with soda water or plain water, and the icing sugar here is optional. Because fresh juice does not keep well, the recipes given here are sufficient for one glass only. However, if you want to prepare it in larger quantities, one standard bottle of juice can be obtained by trebling the amount of ingredients in each recipe and increasing the amount of water to make up the bulk. To preserve the juice, add one powdered Camden tablet per bottle, and sterilise the bottles before use by soaking in a Camden solution or by immersing in boiling water. Use screw-top glass bottles if you intend using the juice within a few days and store in a cool place, preferably a refrigerator. If you want to keep the juice longer, use screw-top plastic bottles and store in the icebox.

large cucumber	half
water	5 fl. ozs (142 ml)
icing sugar	2 teaspoons
salt	

1. Peel and chop the cucumber.
2. Put the cucmber in the liquidiser along with the water, icing sugar and a pinch of salt.
3. Liquidise, pour into a glass and serve immediately.

PARSNIP JUICE

These fruit and vegetable drinks can be made either with soda water or plain water, and the icing sugar here is optional. Because fresh juice does not keep well, the recipes given here are sufficient for one glass only. However, if you want to prepare it in larger quantities, one standard bottle of juice can be obtained by trebling the amount of ingredients in each recipe and increasing the amount of water to make up the bulk. To preserve the juice, add one powdered Camden tablet per bottle, and sterilise the bottles before use by soaking in a Camden solution or by immersing in boiling water. Use screw-top glass bottles if you intend using the juice within a few days and store in a cool place, preferably a refrigerator. If you want to keep the juice longer, use screw-top plastic bottles and store in the icebox.

parsnips	2 medium
water	5 fl. ozs (142 ml)
icing sugar	1 teaspoon
fresh pineapple	1 slice

1. Scrape and chop the parsnips.
2. Put the parsnips in the liquidiser along with the water, icing sugar and pineapple slice.
3. Liquidise, pour into a glass and serve immediately.

TOMATO JUICE

These fruit and vegetable drinks can be made either with soda water or plain water, and the icing sugar here is optional. Because fresh juice does not keep well, the recipes given here are sufficient for one glass only. However, if you want to prepare it in larger quantities, one standard bottle of juice can be obtained by trebling the amount of ingredients in each recipe and increasing the amount of water to make up the bulk. To preserve the juice, add one powdered Camden tablet per bottle, and sterilise the bottles before use by soaking in a Camden solution or by immersing in boiling water. Use screw-top glass bottles if you intend using the juice within a few days and store in a cool place, preferably a refrigerator. If you want to keep the juice longer, use screw-top plastic bottles and store in the icebox.

ripe tomatoes	3
water	5 fl. ozs (142 ml)
icing sugar	1 teaspoon
salt	
worcester sauce	

1. Dip three large ripe tomatoes into boiling water for a moment to loosen the skin and peel.
2. Put the tomatoes in the liquidiser along with the water, icing sugar, a pinch of salt and a dash of Worcester sauce.
3. Liquidise, pour into a glass and serve immediately.

HERB TEAS (OR TISANES)

Though made in a tea-pot, these are not strictly teas (tea being a herb in its own right), but infusions of various herbs more correctly called tisanes. This old French name was originally given to decoctions used in folk medicine, and herb 'teas' are still used today for medicinal purposes as well as being enjoyed simply as pleasant and refreshing drinks.

Fresh herbs can be used – mint, sage and lemon balm in particular – but tisanes are generally best made with dried herbs. The following are most commonly used:

lemon balm
lemon verbena
lovage
mint (especially catmint, peppermint, eau de cologne, lemon and pineapple mints)
rosemary
sage
savory
thyme (especially lemon thyme)

1. The method of drying is important, to ensure that the herb retains as much of its natural colour and flavour as possible. Gather just before flowering, when the flavour is strongest, and take only the young growing tips. Small-leaved herbs such as thyme and rosemary can be left on the stalk, but larger-leaved ones such as mint and sage should be stripped off.
2. Spread the leaves out on a sheet of thin paper on a wire rack – a cake rack is fine – and leave in a warm place, for instance an airing cupboard or a sunny window sill, turning them frequently so that they dry evenly.

3. The herbs are ready when the leaves crumble between the fingers. Crush them coarsely (don't reduce them to a powder or you'll have difficulty straining the tea) and store in an air-tight tin or a sealed polythene bag.
4. For each cup of herb tea, use 1 teaspoon of dried crushed leaves, or 1 tablespoon of fresh chopped leaves. Add the leaves to a warmed tea-pot, cover with boiling water, stir and leave to infuse for 5 minutes before straining into cups. It's usual to add 1–2 teaspoons of freshly-squeezed lemon or orange juice, and sugar according to individual taste. 'Teas' can also be made in this way from other leaves, and some blossom, including dandelion leaf, raspberry leaf, alfalfa leaf, lime blossom and red clover.

FURTHER READING

First Steps in Winemaking, CJJ Berry (Fox Chapel Publishing, 2011)
Making Wines Like Those You Buy, Bryan Acton & Peter Duncan
(Special Interest Model Books, 1998)
The Wine and Beer Maker's Year, Roy Elkins (Special Interest Model
Books, 2000)
Making Sparkling Wines, John Restall & David Hobbs (Fox Chapel
Publishing, 2012)
Kit Wine Making, Daniel Pambianchi (Vehicule Press, 2009)
Growing Vines to make Wines, N. Poulter (Vehicule Press, 2009)
Home Brewing – a Guide to Making Your Own Beer, Wine, and Cider,
Ted Bruning (National Trust Books, 2011)

PICTURE CREDITS

INDEX I

INDEX II